W9-BVJ-051

Taiwan

Taiwan

BY BARBARA A. SOMERVILL

Enchantment of the World™
Second Series

CHILDREN'S PRESS®

An Imprint of Scholastic Inc.

New York   Toronto   London   Auckland   Sydney
Mexico City   New Delhi   Hong Kong
Danbury, Connecticut

Frontispiece: **Temple at Sun Moon Lake**

Consultant: Joseph R. Allen, Chair, Department of Asian Languages and Literatures, University of Minnesota, Minneapolis
Please note: All statistics are as up-to-date as possible at the time of publication.

Book production by The Design Lab

Library of Congress Cataloging-in-Publication Data
Somervill, Barbara A.
 Taiwan / by Barbara A. Somervill.
 pages cm.—(Enchantment of the world)
 Includes bibliographical references and index.
 ISBN 978-0-531-22018-4 (lib. bdg.)
 1. Taiwan—Juvenile literature. I. Title.
 DS799.S59 2014
 951.249—dc23   2013023422

1 2 3 4 5 6 7 8 9 10 R 23 22 21 20 19 18 17 16 15 14

Dragon Boat Festival in Kaohsiung

Contents

Left to right: **Buddhists praying, Sun Moon Lake, Lantern Festival, Jiufen, Taoist mask**

CHAPTER 1

Home Run!

IT HAD BEEN A TOUGH TOURNAMENT FOR THE LITTLE League baseball team from Taitung County, Taiwan. The players had been struggling. Next up, they faced a hard-hitting team from Caguas, Puerto Rico, and had to win two games to advance to the finals. In the first game, the Taiwanese pitcher hurled a nearly perfect game, and the team won 12–0. The second game saw Taiwan pull ahead early and win 11–5.

The tournament was being played in San Francisco, California. At home in Taiwan, thousands of miles away on the other side of the Pacific Ocean, fans stayed glued to the television. In the finals of the 2012 Bronco League World Series, the Taitung County team battled a team from El Dorado Hills, California. In the final game, Taiwan's team scored eleven runs to El Dorado Hills' five. The victory was sweet. It had been sixteen years since a Taiwan team had won the title.

Opposite: **A Taiwan player throws a pitch during the Little League World Series. Taiwan is among the world's most successful nations in youth baseball competitions.**

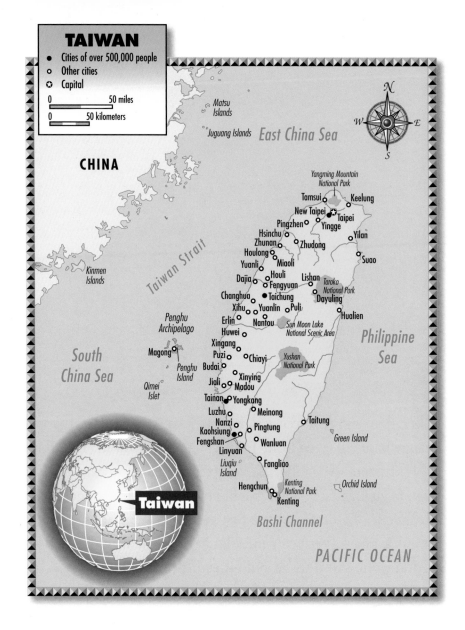

Baseball is wildly popular in Taiwan, a nation officially called the Republic of China. Taiwan occupies the large island of Taiwan and many nearby smaller islands. The main island lies 112 miles (180 kilometers) off the southeast coast of the People's Republic of China, commonly known as China. It is south of Japan and north of the Philippines.

Taiwan is home to many aboriginal, or native, cultures. The ancestors of today's Taiwanese aborigines began arriving there at least five thousand years ago. Beginning in the 1400s, there was contact between the people of Taiwan and the people of China. In the following centuries many people from southeastern China immigrated to the island. They brought with them their language and culture.

In 1895, following a war between Japan and China, Taiwan was given to Japan. The Japanese introduced baseball to the island. They also exploited the island, using its farmland to

Many different aborigine groups live in Taiwan. At one time, Taiwanese aborigines spoke about twenty-five different languages. Today, only fifteen of these languages are still spoken.

A Japanese man (right) with a native of Taiwan (left). The Japanese ruled Taiwan for nearly fifty years.

produce the rice and sugar it needed. Japanese control of Taiwan ended with the Japanese defeat in World War II (1939–1945). Control of Taiwan was given to General Chiang Kai-shek, the leader of the Chinese Nationalists. He was struggling against communists led by Mao Zedong for control of China. In 1949, the communists won the Chinese Civil War, and Chiang Kai-shek and about two million other Chinese fled to Taiwan.

Today, Taiwan has a strong element of Chinese culture, but Taiwanese aborigine and Japanese cultures also have an influence. It is a land of densely packed cities, thriving industries, and towering mountains. People in Taiwan both hold on to their cultural traditions and are at the center of the modern world. They also love baseball.

Local baseball games at all levels draw enthusiastic crowds. On Saturday afternoons in July, parents and friends fill the stands to support their favorite Little Leaguers. They cheer noisily for every hit and groan over every strike out. At professional games, crowd approval can be deafening and dramatic. When the Uni-President Lions, a team from Tainan, win a home game, orange streamers pour out of the stands and cover the field like a mass of carrot-colored spaghetti. Nothing draws Taiwanese sports fans quite like the home team on a field of dreams.

The Uni-President Lions celebrate winning the league championship in 2009.

CHAPTER 2

Many Mountains

I T IS LATE SPRING, AND LI JIA-HAO PLANS TO GO mountain climbing on Yu, Taiwan's tallest mountain. Five hours from his home in Taipei, the capital, he joins a climbing group. The trekkers camp overnight and head up the trail at daybreak. The morning's warm temperatures and mist give way to chilly air and a view of rugged peaks and mountain forests. The group stops for lunch and camps early in the afternoon. Within an hour of setting up the tents, rain pours down, heavy and cold.

Dawn brings brilliant sunlight and a view so stunning that the rainfall is quickly forgotten. Li Jia-hao takes out his camera and snaps a shot of a Formosan serow, a goatlike animal, munching on tender meadow grasses. In the sparse conifers, he spots a pair of Formosan firecrests, small birds with shrill, sharp songs.

Opposite: **Many streams rush down mountains and through forests in Taiwan.**

Cliffs drop straight into the bright blue water along the east coast of Taiwan.

By late morning, the trekkers reach the crest of the mountain. The air is crisp, the vegetation is stunted by the constant cold and wind, and the view reveals a magnificent cluster of snow-covered peaks in the distance. The island is dominated by five long mountain ranges, which feature 164 peaks that rise higher than 9,800 feet (3,000 meters).

An Island Nation

Taiwan is a collection of one large and many small islands in the western Pacific Ocean. The western coastline of Taiwan lies along the Taiwan Strait. Beyond the strait is China. To the north is the East China Sea, which separates Taiwan from Japan. To the southwest of Taiwan lies the South China Sea. Directly to the south is the Luzon Strait, with the Philippines beyond. The Philippine Sea lies to the east of Taiwan. In addition to the main island of Taiwan, the nation governs clusters of smaller islands, including the Penghu Islands, Green Island, and Orchid Island.

The main island of Taiwan is shaped like a sweet potato. It measures 236 miles (380 km) long and 89 miles (143 km) wide. Five parallel mountain ranges fill most of the island. The westernmost range forms a boundary between the heavily populated western region and the rest of the island.

Geologic History

Taiwan lies on the boundary of tectonic plates, giant pieces of rock that fit together to make up the earth's outer layer. These plates are always slowly moving. Taiwan and its neighboring islands were formed as these plates collided, forcing land beneath the sea upward.

The land along tectonic plate boundaries tends to be geologically active. The land continues to slip, slide, and shift, producing many earthquakes that range from tiny rattles to devastating quakes that crush buildings. In the twentieth century, Taiwan suffered seventeen magnitude 7 earthquakes. These are major earthquakes that are very likely to cause damage. A 7.6 quake struck early on September 21, 1999, killing 2,415 people, injuring 11,305 others, and destroying more than fifty thousand buildings.

Regions that are prone to earthquakes sometimes experience other types of geologic activity such as mud volcanoes and hot springs. The badlands region of southern Taiwan is like a moonscape. Thick slabs of mudstone, carved by wind and water erosion, have created steep slopes, strange shapes, and deep gullies. Mud pools burp beside milky-white alkaline springs. In the Water and Fire Cave near Tainan City, in southwestern Taiwan, bubbles of hot methane pop up and burst into fire through the mud and mist.

Guests take a mud bath at a hot spring in Tainan.

Hills and Mountains

Natural boundaries divide Taiwan into distinct regions. The western region features rolling hills and flat plains. Much of this region is densely populated, with one city blending into the next. The west is also the center of Taiwanese agriculture, and large quantities of rice and other crops are grown there. Along the coastline, tidal flats and wetlands form around the river basins and estuaries near the Taiwan Strait.

The western region ends with the foothills of the mountain ranges that fill the central region of the island. The dominant range is the Zhongyang, or Central Mountain Range, which runs nearly the entire length of the island, dividing it in half.

Taiwan's Geographic Features

Area: 13,855 square miles (35,884 sq km)

Highest Elevation: Mount Yu, 12,966 feet (3,952 m) above sea level

Lowest Elevation: Sea level along the coast

Longest River: Zhuoshui River, 116 miles (187 km)

Longest Mountain Range: Zhongyang (Central Mountain Range), 170 miles (270 km)

Longest Valley: Taitung (East Rift) Valley, 112 miles (180 km)

Largest Lake: Riyue (Sun Moon) Lake, 3 square miles (8 sq km)

Tallest Waterfall: Jiaolong (Dragon Falls) drops about 2,000 feet (600 m)

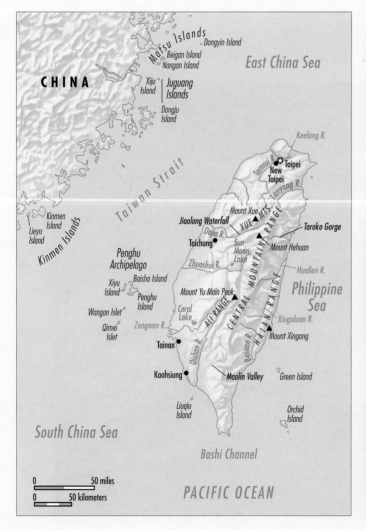

West of the Central Mountain Range, in the north-central part of the island, lie the Xue Mountains, or Snow Mountains. Fifty-four peaks in the Xue rise above 9,800 feet (3,000 m), and many remain snowcapped well into late spring.

To the southwest, the Yu range contains Taiwan's highest peak, also named Yu, or Jade Mountain. It rises to 12,966 feet (3,952 m). The rugged Yu range consists of steep, wooded cliffs, plunging gorges, and a sea of clouds that covers the mountains like whipped cream. Mount Yu itself is not just

The jagged peaks of Mount Yu are often covered in snow.

one peak. Rather, it is a group of ten peaks. Even the lowest of the Yu peaks rises above 9,800 feet (3,000 m).

In the east, the Haian Range hugs the coastline. The mountains are lower than in any of Taiwan's other ranges. The tallest peak, Xingang, rises only 5,518 feet (1,682 m). The Haian Range has sweeping valleys and grasslands, and much of the land is used for agriculture.

The southern end of the Zhongyang becomes the Ali Range, which dips down toward the sea at Taiwan's southernmost tip. The government has dedicated a portion of this range for a National Forest Recreation Area. The area has stunning mountains, broad valleys, and a sea of clouds that glow red and gold at sunrise and sunset.

Surfing is popular in Kenting, along the southern tip of Taiwan.

Beaches and Cities

Taiwan's southern region features the island's most stunning beaches, particularly in Kenting. Here, divers can see abundant brilliantly colored fish swimming near coral reefs. Forests of tangled mangrove trees rise from the water along the coast. The mangroves provide protected areas where young birds and fish can take shelter and grow.

Looking at Taiwan's Cities

New Taipei, the largest city in Taiwan with an estimated population in 2012 of 3,913,595, is literally a new city. It is made up of twenty-nine districts surrounding the capital city, or Taipei City. Previously, these districts were suburbs of Taipei, but in 2010 they combined to become an independent city with its own government. The city has several lively night markets where the locals dine in the evening. Each market has a specialty. Xingnan offers shaved-ice desserts, while diners at Xinzhuang feast on mushroom and meatball stew.

Kaohsiung, in southern Taiwan, is Taiwan's second-largest city, with a population of 2,773,885. It is a transportation hub, home to a large international airport and a seaport with more than a hundred docks. Kaohsiung is a major industrial city, but it also draws many tourists to such sites as the Dragon and Tiger Pagodas (below). Visitors enter the temple through the mouth of the dragon, experience the vivid Chinese artwork along the walkway, and exit through the tiger's mouth.

Taichung (above), the third-largest city, with a population of 2,662,770, is located in western Taiwan. It is remote for such a large metropolitan area and did not have an international airport until 2004. Taichung is an industrial city with many small and midsized factories. It also has thirteen universities and several museums, including the National Museum of Natural Science where visitors enjoy dinosaur exhibits, science and technology halls, the Taiwan Museum of Fine Arts, and a botanical garden.

Taipei, the capital city, is the fourth-largest city, with a population of 2,647,122. The fifth-largest city is Tainan, with a population 1,876,706. Tainan is Taiwan's oldest city, and today it is a mix of the old and the new. Tainan is a city of temples. The Sacrificial Rites Martial Temple is dedicated to Guan Gong, the god of war. Its outstanding feature is an extensive hallway built to resemble the rolling back of a warhorse. Another major temple, the Grand Mazu Temple, honors the goddess of the seas.

At the opposite end of Taiwan, the northern region is heavily populated and full of beaches where Taiwanese people spend summer days enjoying sun and surf. The north's Pacific coast beaches begin a string of unspoiled coastal bays and inlets along the eastern coast. Most of the east, like the mountain regions, has plenty of forestland, along with wetlands and grasslands.

Outlying Islands

Taiwan governs a number of other, much smaller islands. Just off the eastern coast of Taiwan are Green Island and Orchid Island. Green Island, also called Ludao, is a vacation destination. Visitors can relax in one of the only hot springs in the world fed by seawater or dive along the island's coral reefs. At one point, Green Island held several prisons that were specifically for political prisoners. Today, it is a human rights memorial park.

Orchid Island, or Lanyu, lies 40 miles (65 km) southeast of Taiwan. The island has high mountains and deep valleys. Orchid Island is home to the Tao people, Taiwanese aborigines who live in six small villages.

The Penghu Islands are an archipelago, or island chain, that lies west of Taiwan, in the Taiwan Strait. The sixty-four islands in this chain are flat, and the surrounding waters are shallow and warm. The islands are cut with small inlets and bays. Offshore, the warm water provides a good habitat for coral reefs. About 70 percent of the people in the Penghu Islands live on Penghu Island itself. The remaining people live on twenty nearby islands. The major islands are connected by a series of low bridges.

A Taiwanese soldier stands guard in the Matsu Islands. The islands are home to about eight thousand people.

Taiwan also controls several other small archipelagos. Kinmen archipelago consists of twelve islands slightly more than 1 mile (1.6 km) off China's Fujian Province. Matsu, another archipelago, is a string of thirty-six islands with rugged hills. Matsu lies next to the mouth of China's Min River, less than a mile from mainland Asia. The control of these islands has caused friction between Taiwan and China, particularly because Taiwan stations army troops on Matsu and Kinmen.

Rivers and Lakes

Taiwan is blessed with plentiful freshwater. About 150 rivers flow down from the mountains. Most of Taiwan's rivers have short, steep courses, with rushing water and plenty of rapids. During the rainy season, the flow increases, and many rivers carry large amounts of silt, gravel, and soil, which they dump at the river's mouth. The rivers provide freshwater for drinking and crop irrigation, and some are used for kayaking and whitewater rafting.

The Zhuoshui in central Taiwan is the nation's longest river, at 116 miles (187 km). The river that is most easily navigated is the Tamsui, which passes through Taipei and empties into the sea near the district of Tamsui. The Tamsui River has been used to transport rice, sugar, coal, and tea leaves from inland to the sea. Once a nesting site for water and wading birds, this river now suffers from heavy pollution. The government has recently begun a project to clean up the Tamsui and rebuild the river's beaches and wetlands.

There are few natural lakes in Taiwan. The largest is Riyue Lake, or Sun Moon Lake, in the Yu Mountains. Most other lakes in Taiwan are either smaller mountain lakes or artificial lakes formed by river dams.

Taroko National Park

Among the most remarkable natural sites in Taiwan is Taroko Gorge, which lies near Hualien in the eastern part of the island. From high in the mountains, the Liwu River carves a blue-green path eastward through dramatic marble walls and patches of densely covered woodland. In places, the narrow road passes through tunnels cut in a mountainside. From above the gorge, waterfalls splash into the water far below. Visitors enjoy natural waterslides, stunning wildflowers, hot springs, and varied wildlife, including Taiwan macaques, goat-like serows, and Formosan black bears.

Hot, Cold, Rainy, Dry

Taiwan has widely diverse terrain and a varied climate to match. Monsoons, high temperatures, dry winters, snowy mountains, and sticky humidity are all common.

Taiwan's hot season lasts from April or May until October. The cold season, which is not all that cold, lasts from November to March or April. It can—and does—rain at any time.

In Taipei, in the north of Taiwan, the average daily high temperature year-round is 80 degrees Fahrenheit (27 degrees Celsius). Tainan and other parts of southern Taiwan are even hotter. There, the average daily high temperature is 84°F

People walk down steps in Jiufen, in northern Taiwan. In the winter, the northern part of Taiwan receives more rain than the southern part.

(29°C). July is the warmest month, with average daily high temperatures in Taipei soaring to 94°F (34°C), with plenty of sticky humidity. Temperatures are significantly colder in the mountains, where snow falls in the winter at high elevations.

Rainfall on the main island of Taiwan is plentiful. The average annual precipitation is about 102 inches (259 centimeters), although some parts of Taiwan receive more than 200 inches (about 500 cm) of rain in a single summer. Mountain ranges form a barrier between east and west and block heavy rainfall from sweeping across the island. Because of this, eastern Taiwan gets more rain than western Taiwan. Northern winters tend to be drizzly, while southern winters are dry and sunny. Major storms called typhoons are most common in July, August, and September, when Taiwan gets its heaviest precipitation.

CHAPTER 3

From Monkeys to Magpies

TAIWAN IS ONE OF THE MOST DENSELY POPULATED countries on Earth. The people of Taiwan need land for housing, industry, farming, and roads. This has harmed the native plant and animal population of the country. Until recent decades, conserving nature in Taiwan came a distant second to human needs.

During the twentieth century, efforts to preserve the unique and varied ecosystems of the island were mostly ignored. But in more recent years, the government and conservationists have created a plan to preserve ecosystems, establish nature parks and sanctuaries, and protect Taiwan's endangered species. To slow the loss of forestland and protect endangered species, Taiwan established the Central Mountain Green Corridor. This region consists of a series of protected ecosystems, including nineteen nature reserves, fourteen wildlife refuges, and twenty-eight major protected wildlife habitats.

Opposite: **Formosan rock macaques are the only monkey species native to Taiwan. They typically live in mountainous forests and grasslands.**

The King of the Trees

Safeguarding Taiwan's forests is not just the work of the government. Lai Pei-yuan is a Taiwanese businessman who made a fortune in transportation and is using his money to replant deforested mountainsides. He has become known as the King of the Trees. Lai buys thousands of trees each year, which he and an army of volunteers plant near Taichung. So far, more than 270,000 trees have been planted on a mountainside where many trees had been harvested. Lai's tree-planting troops have created a forest of native Taiwanese species, including incense cedar and cinnamomum trees. Says Lai, "It was just a simple idea I had. If I was to safeguard Taiwan, I would have to plant trees."

Unusual Mammals

Few large mammals live in Taiwan, but most that do are endemic, meaning they do not live anywhere else. The island's largest mammal is the Formosan black bear. Weighing between 100 and 400 pounds (45 and 180 kilograms), Formosan black bears roam the mountain forests of Taiwan. Shy and skittish, the bears have white bibs on their chests and doglike snouts. The bears eat just about anything, from fruits and roots to insects and decaying animal flesh.

Other mammals that live in Taiwan are Formosan Reeves's muntjacs, clouded leopards, and Formosan macaques. Muntjacs are short, squat deer that weigh about 30 pounds (14 kg). Taiwan's clouded leopard population may no longer exist, although there is a chance that a few individual cats survive in remote mountain areas. While the clouded leopard

A red giant flying squirrel glides through the air, using the loose skin between its limbs to form a kite.

is rare, Formosan macaques are so plentiful and devilish that they have become a serious problem to farmers. They shout, scream, and steal crops.

The nation's smaller mammals include mice, rats, bats, otters, martens, and some wild cats. Taiwan has several varieties of civets, small weasel-like creatures that live in grasslands, woodlands, and rain forests. It is also home to a species of giant flying squirrel, a red-and-white nocturnal animal that launches itself from treetops and coasts to neighboring trees.

Birds Aplenty

Taiwan's forests, mangroves, wetlands, and meadows provide nesting and feeding grounds for about five hundred species of birds. Many species of migratory birds use Taiwan as a stopover between their summer and winter nesting grounds. A total of 5 percent of the world's bird species live in or pass through Taiwan.

Species in Danger: Formosan Flying Fox

A flying fox is not a fox at all, although its face looks somewhat foxlike. The Formosan flying fox is actually a giant bat. Formosan flying foxes have a wingspan of slightly more than 3 feet (1 m) and feed on nectar, blossoms, pollen, and fruit. Most bats use echoloca- tion—the reflection of sound waves—to find food. But flying foxes have well-developed senses of sight and smell. Scientists thought these bats were on the brink of extinction, but in 2010 conservationists found a group of the bats on Turtle Mountain Island.

The island has fifteen bird species found only in Taiwan. The two best known are the Formosan blue magpie and the Mikado pheasant. The blue magpie is Taiwan's national bird, and the Mikado pheasant appears on the New Taiwan $1,000 bill. Other forest birds that live only in Taiwan include Swinhoe's pheasants, Taiwan hill partridges, and Taiwan firecrests. A firecrest is a tiny bird that lives at high altitudes in evergreen forests. A vivid yellow and orange crest makes the firecrest look like it has flames on its head. Taiwan's most remarkable-looking bird is the fairy pitta,

The male Mandarin duck is brightly colored, and the female is brown.

which is nicknamed the eight-color bird because of its multicolored feathers of shining red, green, and blue.

The black-faced spoonbill uses its long bill to scoop up fish.

Wading birds, such as black-faced spoonbills and Chinese egrets, thrive in Taiwan's salt marshes and mangroves. Ibises and storks dip their bills into the shallow marsh waters to feast on tiny shrimp and minnows. Mandarin ducks, another rare species,

National Bird

The Formosan blue magpie travels in groups of three to ten individuals, particularly in mating season. They live in lowland forests and feed on large insects, small birds, bird eggs, rats, frogs, lizards, and fruit. With a black neck and head, brilliant blue body feathers, and a splash of white on the tail, these birds are easily identified. In 2007, the people of Taiwan voted for an official national bird, and the Formosan blue magpie won. It has not yet been adopted as the official national bird, though.

paddle in local ponds and marshes. The males have distinctive bright rust-red bills, and slashes of white, black, and red feathers.

Several birds of prey call Taiwan home. Ospreys swoop down to pluck fish from the water, while quick-flying peregrine falcons catch birds in flight. There are eagles, owls, hawks, and buzzards to round out the roster of predatory birds. Predators help keep small bird and rodent populations under control.

Watch Where You Walk

Hikers need to pay close attention to where they walk in Taiwan. They need to stay on the paths, because Taiwan has several species of vipers and cobras that hide among rocks, woods, and water. Particularly dangerous are Taiwan banded kraits. Their venom can cause death within two hours if not treated.

The Taiwan banded krait grows up to 6 feet (1.8 m) long.

Bamboo vipers, Taiwan's most common venomous snakes, relax in trees and strike from heights. The hundred-pacer snake, a pit viper, gets its name because legend says that, once bitten, the victim will not make it one hundred paces before dying. Taiwan is also home to many nonvenomous snakes, including the greater green snake and the collared reed snake.

Frogs and toads enjoy wet weather, making Taiwan's climate ideal for amphibians. Most frogs and toads are nocturnal. They live along the edge of lakes and slow rivers, in streams and rice paddies, in stands of bamboo, and in trees. Taiwan's frogs struggle in a land with so many people, cars, and trucks. Sauter's brown frog, which lives only in Taiwan, crosses roads at night to reach its breeding ground. Traffic is heavy, and many frogs get squashed. To help preserve this species, two hundred volunteers gather in October—mating season—to collect the frogs from the Hsinchu wilderness and hand deliver them in safety to the stream where they breed.

Many tree frogs live in Taiwan. Male frogs push large amounts of air into their vocal sacs to make loud sounds.

Creepy Crawlies

Insects dominate the list of animal species in Taiwan. The island hosts eighteen thousand insect species, including Formosan giant stag beetles and brilliant jewel beetles. Giant stag beetles can be anywhere from 1 to 3 inches (2.5 to 8 cm) long. They are black, fierce, and look like aliens from outer space. Jewel beetles have shimmering, metallic-looking backs in shades of red and bright green. Taiwanese aborigines have used their shells for decorating clothing and jewelry.

Many butterflies also brighten the landscape in Taiwan. The highland red-bellied swallowtail is a large, colorful butterfly with a wingspan of 5 inches (13 cm). The purple crow butterfly migrates between low-altitude gorges in the Maolin Valley in southern Taiwan. During migration time, hundreds of thousands of butterflies pass through the area, including such colorfully named creatures as dwarf crows, double-branded black crows, and chocolate tigers.

One of the largest of Taiwan's insects is the big-headed giant stick insect. Found in Kenting National Park, these huge insects look like long, thin branches. They are so well camouflaged that they can only be seen when they are moving. Some of these giant insects measure more than 12 inches (30 cm) long.

Another startling creature common in Taiwan is the Taiwan centipede. These many-legged creatures are sometimes 6 inches (15 cm) long.

The highland red-bellied swallowtail lives only in Taiwan.

Towering red cypress trees in Alishan National Scenic Area draw many visitors.

Growing on the Land

Taiwan's plant life is similar to the plants found in neighboring China and the Philippines. More than 3,800 plant species live on the islands. Coastal areas have varieties of palms, mangroves, and marsh reeds. From sea level up to about 6,600 feet (2,000 m), tropical evergreen forests, bamboo forests, and a mix of palms, teaks, pistaches, and oaks are common. Above that altitude, pines, firs, spruces, and junipers dominate the landscape. In the mountains, even sheer cliffs support stands of scrawny Taiwan pines. In rain forests, giant cypress trees draw everyone's attention.

In the south, tropical palms, dangling vines, banyan trees, and acacia trees thrive. Bright red hibiscus blooms flare like flames amid the plants' dark green leaves. Wild azaleas sprinkle reds and pinks in wilderness areas. In the lowland areas, evergreen oaks spread their branches and provide shade against the hot summer sun.

In colder regions, mountain slopes support a variety of pine, cypress, and juniper trees. Amid the dark greens, wild rhododendrons blossom with

vivid pink flowers. Lacy ferns grow beside rushing streams, along with many types of moss and lichens.

Flowers have a long tradition in the history and artistry of Taiwan, and no flower is as closely linked to Taiwan as the orchid. Taiwan has been called the kingdom of orchids because of the many species that originated in its rain-drenched forests. Most of these delicate, butterfly-like blooms are grown now on flower farms and make up the basis of Taiwan's multibillion-dollar flower industry.

National Parks and Preserves

In recent decades, Taiwan has established natural parks and preserves to protect its natural wonders from destruction. Today, Taiwan has eight national parks, including Yangming Mountain, Kenting, Yushan, and Taroko. They protect some of Taiwan's most beautiful and threatened environments.

In Taiwan, conservation efforts have expanded beyond the shore and into the surrounding waters. Coral are tiny marine creatures that live together in vast colonies. Coral reefs are

Tourists travel to Taroko National Park to see the gnarled trees and spectacular scenery.

made up of the skeletons of the coral. These reefs provide an important habitat for fish and other sea creatures. Young fish can hide among the colorful coral, safe from predators. Recently, Taiwan surveyed the condition of its coral reefs. It was determined that the reefs needed to be protected, both for their own sake and for the sea life that depends on them.

The country's largest reef system is near Green Island. Marine biologists have found that a disease is turning the coral black, as if a thin black cloth were slowly covering the coral colonies. Called black death, this disease stops needed sunlight from reaching the coral, killing it. The loss of coral eventually results in the loss of fish species, which Taiwan needs for survival. Humphead wrasse, parrotfish, and reef barracuda can no longer be found at the reef sites investigated. Aquarium fish, such as butterfly fish, are also low in numbers. The government plans to protect Green Island's reef, but scientists are not sure what can be done to stop the invading black death.

As the government has passed laws to clean up the air and water, private groups have cleaned up beaches and replanted forests. Laws have been passed requiring that people pay for plastic bags when they shop. This encourages people to bring reusable bags to shops and sends less plastic to the dump. Taiwan has made great strides in controlling pollution in recent years, and the people of Taiwan hope to continue to improve the health of their environment.

Eco-friendly Art

Cheng Long Wetlands is in Taiwan's poorest region. Most of the people who live around the wetlands preserve survive by farming fish or rice. In 2011, artist Huang Hsin-yu introduced the idea of creating an eco-friendly art gallery in the wetlands. Five internationally known artists joined Huang in producing large, dramatic artworks using driftwood, local grasses, and materials such as recycled bamboo from old oyster beds. In 2013, artists moved into the village again and began creating new works of art in Cheng Long. The artworks remain on display for one year or until they decompose, whichever comes first.

CHAPTER 4

A Rich History

E VIDENCE SUGGESTS THAT HUMAN BEINGS BEGAN settling the island of Taiwan about thirty thousand years ago. Archaeologists, people who study the remains of past cultures, have investigated many early settlements, but they still know very little about Taiwan's earliest inhabitants. They do know that these earliest people are not related to Taiwan's current aborigine groups.

The Dapenkeng culture arose between 4000 BCE and 3000 BCE. They are believed to be the ancestors of today's Taiwanese aborigines. They spoke languages related to those spoken on Southeast Asian and Pacific islands. Over time, the settlers spread inland away from the coast. Different groups developed different cultures and languages. Archaeologists have discovered tombs, weapons, bronze tools, bits of pottery, and shell mounds from these early settlers. These sites offer clues about the lives of early Taiwanese people, but they do not tell a complete story.

Opposite: **A Bunun carving towers among the trees near Sun Moon Lake.**

Sun Quan founded the Eastern Wu dynasty.

Exploring the Island

The first mention of Taiwan in recorded history was in 206 BCE. At the time, the Han dynasty ruled China, and the emperor sent an expedition to explore the nearby islands. Some historians believe that the island that they named Yangzhou was Taiwan.

By 229 CE, the Eastern Wu controlled southern China. The Eastern Wu had many skilled sailors, and the emperor built shipyards to support the interest in travel. Legend has it that in 239, Emperor Sun Quan sent ten thousand people to settle Taiwan. It is extremely unlikely that this is true. For another thousand years, little was heard about Taiwan.

Era of the Chinese Dragon Ships

In the 1400s, the Chinese navigator Zheng He set sail in a ship decorated with giant dragon eyes in the prow. According to legend, Zheng sailed across the China Sea and perhaps as far as the East African coast. Zheng had almost no sailing experience, but he did have the support of the emperor Zhu Di.

Zhu Di, also known as the Yongle emperor, was the third emperor of the Ming dynasty. He was fascinated by foreign lands and wanted to expand his empire. He chose a bright yellow five-clawed dragon to represent his rule, and the symbol appeared on his ships.

It is said that a great storm drove Zheng He's ships to the island of Taiwan. Like many other explorers, Zheng took credit for discovering a place that had been inhabited for thousands of years.

Around the same time, pirates were using Taiwan as their base. From the 1300s through the 1500s, pirates sailed from China and southern Japan to prey on merchant ships in the Taiwan Strait. After plundering the wealth of the ships they attacked, the pirates slipped away to Taiwan and out of the reach of the imperial Chinese navy.

A full-size replica of Zheng He's ship sits in a shipyard in Nanjing, China, where his original ship was built.

Outsiders Arrive

In the 1400s and 1500s the Portuguese were among the world's leading explorers. They tried to establish a trading post on the north of Taiwan, which they called Formosa, but it did not succeed.

The Japanese also wanted the island. In 1598, the Japanese ruler Tokugawa sent several thousand men to take over Taiwan and set up a post there. The native Taiwanese people fought to protect their home. Different groups of Taiwanese aborigines usually did not work together, but in this case they presented a united army against the Japanese. Although the aborigines pushed back the Japanese, they were not able to force them completely off the island. Japan's government built a small settlement called Takasago.

In the 1600s, the Dutch East India Company bought and sold spices, herbs, silks, and other goods from Japan, China, and other Southeast Asian locations. These items brought high prices in European cities. In 1622, the Dutch set up a small fort on Penghu Island, and two years later they established settlements on Taiwan.

Portuguese ships sailing in the Indian Ocean. The Portuguese were the first Europeans to sail around the southern tip of Africa and on to Asia.

An Island with Two Names

In the 1500s, the Portuguese sent many ships exploring the world. On their way to Japan in 1590, Portuguese sailors passed the island of Taiwan. They called it *ilha formosa*, "beautiful island" in Portuguese. For nearly five centuries, people in the Western world called the island Formosa. To the Chinese, it was always Taiwan.

The Spanish were also interested in setting up trade agreements with Japan. Spain saw the Dutch as rivals in the Asian trade market. They set up small forts at what are now Keelung and Tamsui. After many aboriginal attacks on their settlements, the Spanish abandoned the Keelung fort. The Dutch now had free access to Taiwan. For years, they tried to take over the entire island, but they never developed more than a few small coastal villages.

The Dutch brought in workers from Fujian, a mountainous region of China. By 1660, there were twenty-five Chinese workers for every Dutch citizen. The Chinese workers cleared land for farming, and profitable crops were introduced. Under the Dutch, sugarcane was grown, and the sugar was sold to the

The Spanish built Fort San Domingo out of wood in 1628. It was damaged in an attack, and they rebuilt it out of stone in 1637. The fort stands in Tamsui, near Taipei.

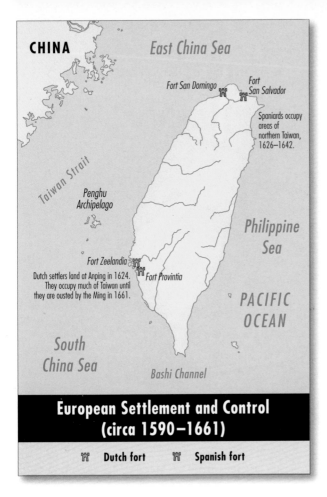

CHINA

East China Sea

Fort San Domingo

Fort San Salvador

Spaniards occupy areas of northern Taiwan, 1626–1642.

Taiwan Strait

Penghu Archipelago

Philippine Sea

Fort Zeelandia

Dutch settlers land at Anping in 1624. They occupy much of Taiwan until they are ousted by the Ming in 1661.

Fort Provintia

PACIFIC OCEAN

South China Sea

Bashi Channel

European Settlement and Control (circa 1590–1661)

Dutch fort Spanish fort

Japanese. People also caught and dried fish, which they sold to the Chinese. Deer meat, skins, and antlers were processed by local hunters and also sold to the Chinese and Japanese. The Dutch charged taxes for growing, processing, and selling these goods. Hunters needed licenses, and paid for them with 10 percent of their goods.

The Era of Koxinga

The Dutch were soon forced from the island. Zheng Chenggong was a talented naval commander. He was faithful to China's Ming rulers. When Qing troops took over in the Fujian region, Zheng swore he would help return the Ming to the throne.

In 1659, he led a military mission with one hundred thousand troops. The group sailed up the Yangtze River to battle the Qing. At first, Zheng's troops enjoyed success, but when additional Qing forces arrived from the south, Zheng's army suffered a serious defeat. In 1661, Zheng went to Taiwan and laid siege to the Dutch fortress at Anping. Nine months later, the Dutch gave up and left the island. Zheng was called Koxinga by the Dutch, and he established Chinese rule in Taiwan.

Zheng wanted Taiwan to have a culture like that of the Ming dynasty. Zheng brought teachers, artists, philosophers, poets, and monks with him to Taiwan. He set up a Chinese style of government, with himself as the leader. Zheng did not get to enjoy his Ming paradise for long. He died a few months after gaining control of Taiwan, and his son took over governing Taiwan.

Meanwhile, the Qing continued to control China, and in 1683, they attacked and gained control of Taiwan. This brought an end to Zheng's rule of the island.

Qing Rule

The Qing ruled Taiwan for several centuries, but it was not a peaceful time there. Uprisings were frequent. The local population regularly rose up to protest taxes, oppression, and brutal laws.

A shrine to Zheng Chenggong in Tainan. He is considered a national hero in Taiwan.

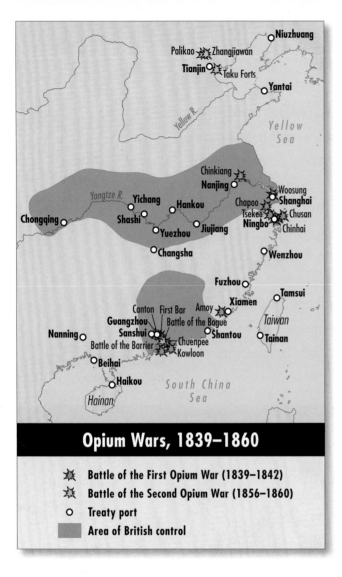

Opium Wars, 1839–1860

- ✳ Battle of the First Opium War (1839–1842)
- ✳ Battle of the Second Opium War (1856–1860)
- ○ Treaty port
- ▨ Area of British control

Although the Qing restricted immigration to Taiwan, large numbers of Chinese immigrants had begun settling in Taiwan in the 1600s anyway. By the end of Zheng's rule, it is estimated that the island's population had grown to about 200,000. Chinese immigrants again streamed in during the late 1700s and early 1800s. By 1842, the island's population was about 2.5 million.

In 1839, China became involved in a series of wars with Great Britain. Called the Opium Wars, they dealt with disagreements over trade laws and diplomacy. China wanted to control trade with the European nations. Until the 1830s, the only Chinese port open to Westerners was Guangzhou. The British used their naval power to invade and control China's ports. They took over much of China's southeastern rice-growing region. As a result of these wars, more Chinese ports were opened to British trade. The 1858 Treaty of Tianjin opened two Taiwanese ports, Tainan and Tamsui, to the British. After this, British trading companies set up offices in Taiwan, and tea became an important export crop.

In 1887, Taiwan became a separate province of China. The first governor of the province, Liu Ming-chuan, set about modernizing the land. He introduced street lighting and ordered Taiwan's first railroad built. Streets were repaved for easier traveling. Liu's railroad provided transportation between Taipei and Keelung.

The Arrival of the Japanese

In 1894, China fought yet another war, this time against Japan. In the treaty that ended the war in 1895, China ceded Taiwan to Japan. The people of Taiwan opposed this treaty. A small group

Taiwanese workers load tea into crates to be shipped overseas. Tea was Taiwan's top export in the late 1800s.

Taiwanese rebels battled Japanese troops in the years after Japan took over Taiwan.

of Taiwanese named their country the Republic of Taiwan, and hoped Western nations would stand up for them. However, the Taiwanese people were disappointed, as this did not happen.

The Japanese arrived with military power. Chinese soldiers and Taiwanese citizens resisted, and more than seven thousand people were killed over the first few months of Japanese occupation.

Compared to Taiwan, Japan was extremely modern. The first changes the Japanese made were improvements in transportation, sanitation, and education. Roads and railroad lines were built to establish easy transportation throughout the island. To improve trade, the Japanese established modern ports in Keelung and Kaohsiung. The Japanese planned to use Taiwan to grow rice and sugar that would be sent to Japan. The Japanese wanted to turn Taiwan into the "kingdom of rice and sugar."

In the 1930s, Japan began trying to change Taiwan from an agricultural economy to an industrial one. Kaohsiung became the site of an aluminum processing plant, power stations, and the light industry. Japanese leaders developed a plan to make Taiwan self-sufficient in industry. By 1939, Taiwan's industrial output exceeded its agricultural output.

Japan entered World War II (1939–1945) on the side of the Axis powers, which included Germany and Italy. Opposing them were the Allies, which included the United States, Great Britain, Russia, and China. Taiwan suffered heavy bombing late in the war because it was part of the Japanese empire.

World War II ended with the surrender of the Japanese on September 2, 1945. Before that time, the Allies held a meeting in Cairo, Egypt. It was agreed that when the war ended, General Chiang Kai-shek's Chinese Nationalist troops would occupy

The Bombing of Taiwan

During World War II, the Japanese relied heavily on air bases and ports in Taiwan to provide military supplies for planes and ships. The island had sixty-five wartime airfields. Sugar mills were used to produce butanol for airplane fuel. Japan's South Strike Group had its base at the Taihoku Imperial University (now National Taiwan University) in Taipei. This made Taiwan a target for American bombers. The U.S. military bombed locations throughout Taiwan, with Linkou, Taipei, and Kaohsiung being prime targets. At one point, bombs struck Taiwan's governor-general's office, and the resulting fire burned for three days.

Taiwan. The Nationalist troops had been fighting communists led by Mao Zedong for control of China. The Chinese occupation of Taiwan was supposed to be a temporary situation, but it did not turn out that way. The Taiwanese people were happy to be rid of their Japanese rulers, but the new Chinese rulers simply replaced the Japanese. Taiwan goods were now being used to support the Chinese Nationalists rather than the Japanese.

In 1949, Chiang Kai-shek lost the civil war in mainland China to the communist forces. He and his troops fled to Taiwan. An estimated two million Chinese fled China for Taiwan during this period. The government of the Republic of China went into exile in Taiwan where it established martial law, a situation where the army makes and enforces the laws.

The White Terror

On February 27, 1947, government agents severely beat a woman in Taipei for selling cigarettes illegally. The beating ignited protests, which spoke to the people's unhappiness over the two years that the Chinese had ruled the island.

General Chiang Kai-shek ordered several thousand troops from mainland China to stop the protests in Taiwan. The troops executed lawyers, students, doctors, professors, and local political leaders. Between eighteen thousand and twenty-eight thousand people were killed. Many more Taiwanese citizens were put in political prisons. This period came to be called the White Terror.

In 1997, commemorating the fiftieth anniversary of this event, people attended a memorial service (right) and displayed photos of the victims.

The Taiwanese people lived under martial law for the next forty years. The Kuomintang (KMT), the party of the Chinese Nationalists, ruled Taiwan.

President Chiang Kai-shek inspects students graduating from service academies in 1970. He dominated Taiwan for decades.

The Postwar Years

Although Chiang Kai-shek and the Nationalists had been forced to retreat to Taiwan, they still claimed that their government, the Republic of China, was the rightful government of all China. Similarly, the communists in China claimed that they ruled all of China, including Taiwan. Because China is so much larger than Taiwan, many people assumed that China would eventually take over the island. But the following decades saw only small clashes. In part, this was because the U.S. government, which opposed communism, protected Taiwan.

Workers put together televisions at a factory in Taipei. Electronics manufacturing boomed in Taiwan beginning in the 1970s.

The United States and some other countries refused to accept the communist government in China as the representatives of the Chinese people. Instead, they accepted Taiwan as the worldwide representative of the Chinese people, and Taiwan was given China's seat in the United Nations. But this situation eventually changed. In 1971, the People's Republic of China took over China's seat in the United Nations, and gradually, the United States developed a relationship with mainland China.

Growth and Change
In the 1960s and 1970s, Taiwan's economy grew rapidly. Exports became increasingly important in Taiwan. The country's factories produced electronics and other goods that were sold in the United States and around the world. The standard of living improved for people in Taiwan.

In time, the political system also changed, becoming more democratic. On July 14, 1987, President Chiang Ching-kuo, who was Chiang Kai-shek's son, announced the end of martial law in Taiwan. The change allowed the formation of new political parties, although the political parties had to oppose communism and support the rejoining of Taiwan and China.

As Taiwan has grown economically, it has improved its ties with China. Taiwan has invested in China, and China has become Taiwan's largest trading partner. Even as China and Taiwan grow closer economically, political issues continue to separate them.

Chiang Ching-kuo became premier of the Republic of China in 1972 and president in 1978.

CHAPTER 5

Governing Taiwan

N 1945, CHIANG KAI-SHEK'S REIGN BEGAN WITH AN "Emergency Decree." Chiang Kai-shek was the supreme ruler and an authoritarian leader. People were allowed to vote, but the only significant party was the Kuomintang (KMT), the Chinese Nationalist Party. Protesters went to prison. Political control could not be questioned.

After Chiang died and his son took office, the tight reins of the Kuomintang gradually eased. In the late 1980s, the Taiwanese people were given the right to demonstrate their political beliefs, form different political parties, and voice their opinions in a free press.

The newly formed Democratic Progressive Party (DPP) was allowed to compete with the Kuomintang for political offices. Other new parties, such as the People First Party, stepped into the political arena.

Opposite: **In the years since martial law ended, Taiwanese people have become increasingly open about expressing their political opinions. Here, people in Taipei protest the policies of President Ma Ying-jeou.**

The Constitution

The constitution of the Republic of China was adopted on December 25, 1946. When it was written, this document was meant to govern both Taiwan and China. For many years, the Republic of China (the government in Taiwan) was recognized as the government of all China by most other nations. As the People's Republic of China (mainland China) began trading with other nations, these nations were compelled to break ties with Taiwan. In 1979, the United States broke off formal diplomatic relations with Taiwan.

The original constitution of the Republic of China set up a one-party system. This ensured that Chiang Kai-shek and the KMT stayed in power. The constitution has been amended, however, so that Taiwan now has a multiparty system. Rather than autocracy, Taiwan now has a democracy in which the people vote for their leaders.

The Three Principles of the People

The constitution of the Republic of China is based on the three principles of the people: nationalism, democracy, and social well-being. These principles were developed by Sun Yat-sen, a revolutionary who helped overthrow the Qing dynasty and found the Republic of China in 1912. The first principle insists on the equal rights for China among other nations and all ethnic groups within the country. The principle of democracy grants Chinese citizens the rights to political and civil liberties. The final principle requires the government to make sure the people enjoy a wealthy, fair society.

The current president of Taiwan is Ma Ying-jeou (below). Ma was first elected to the Legislative Yuan in 1991. He served as the minister of justice from 1993 to 1996, and in 1998 he became the mayor of Taipei. He won the 2008 presidential election by a landslide, when the KMT won 81 of 113 seats in the legislature. In 2012, Ma's campaign centered on improving Taiwan's relationship with China.

Jiang Yi-huah (above) is the current premier of the Executive Yuan. Jiang was educated at National Taiwan University, and at Yale University in the United States. He has been a professor of social sciences and philosophy at National Taiwan University. Jiang entered politics in 2004 as an adviser to the Ministry of Education. He became the minister of the interior in 2009, vice premier in 2012, and premier in 2013.

Taiwan's constitution lists five branches of government, called Yuans. They are the Executive Yuan, or the cabinet; the Legislative Yuan, or the assembly; the Judicial Yuan, or the courts; the Examination Yuan, which runs civil service examinations; and the Control Yuan, which monitors other branches of government.

The president works out of the Presidential Office Building in Taipei. The building, completed in 1919 during the era of Japanese rule, originally held the offices of the governor-general, the Japanese official in charge of Taiwan.

The President

Taiwan has a president and a vice president. The president, Taiwan's head of state and commander in chief of the armed forces, is now directly elected by the people for a four-year term. Both the president and vice president run on the same political ticket, similar to the way the U.S. elects its president and vice president. The president can serve two consecutive terms.

The Executive Yuan

The Executive Yuan is made up of a premier, a vice premier, ministers and commission heads, and political advisers. The president appoints the premier. The remaining members of the Executive Yuan are recommended by the premier and then appointed by the president.

The Executive Yuan has specific responsibilities for leading the government. The council looks over all bills concerned

National Anthem

In 1924, Chinese leader Sun Yat-sen gave a speech at a military academy. This speech became the lyrics to "Zhonghua Minguo guoge," meaning "National Anthem of the Republic of China." Cheng Maoyun wrote the music in 1928. The official English translation of the lyrics uses one Chinese phrase, *San Min Chu-i*, which means "Three Principles of the People." It refers to the ideas of nationalism, democracy, and social well-being developed by Sun Yat-sen.

English translation

San Min Chu-i,
Our aim shall be:
To found a free land,
World peace, be our stand.
Lead on, comrades,
Vanguards ye are.
Hold fast your aim,
By sun and star.
Be earnest and brave,
Your country to save,
One heart, one soul,
One mind, one goal.

with finance, the military, declarations of war, treaties, matters of state, and other important affairs. These bills are then presented to the Legislative Yuan to be passed into law.

The premier's job is to explain the Executive Yuan's policies and decisions to the Legislative Yuan. Any bills that are passed into law must be signed by both the president and the premier.

The Legislative Yuan

Taiwan's Legislative Yuan has 113 members. Most of the members are elected to represent the people of different dis-

A Look at the Capital

Taipei, the capital of Taiwan, lies on the Tamsui River in northern Taiwan. The city has a population of 2,647,122. The city and the surrounding area, known as Greater Taipei, is home to about twelve million people. The area that is now Taipei was first settled by aborigines around 4000 BCE, but the city itself was not founded until the late nineteenth century CE.

Taipei is the center of finance, culture, and education in Taiwan. Highlights of the city include the National Palace Museum, which houses ancient Chinese artifacts, and the Shung Ye Museum of Formosan Aborigines, which displays art and artifacts of the native peoples of Taiwan. The city's most notable landmark is probably Taipei 101, a 101-story skyscraper that was the world's tallest building from 2003 to 2007.

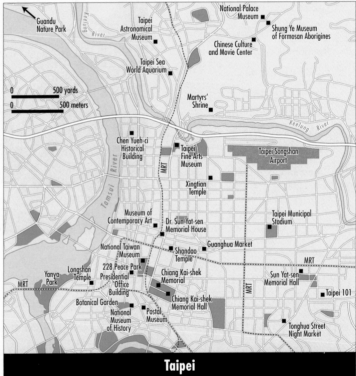

Taipei

tricts. Thirty-four at-large members represent the nation as a whole. They are elected based on the portion of the votes each party receives. Political parties must receive a minimum of 5 percent of the vote to qualify for having any at-large

National Government of Taiwan

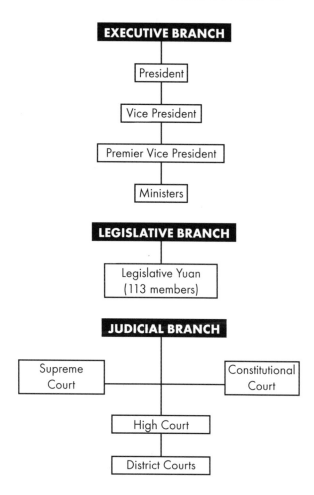

EXECUTIVE BRANCH

President

Vice President

Premier Vice President

Ministers

LEGISLATIVE BRANCH

Legislative Yuan
(113 members)

JUDICIAL BRANCH

Supreme Court

Constitutional Court

High Court

District Courts

members. Aboriginal populations elect another six representatives. Representatives serve for four years.

The KMT and DPP hold the most seats in the Legislative Yuan. Other parties represented in the legislature include the People First Party, the Taiwan Solidarity Union, the Non-Partisan Solidarity Union, and one independent seat.

The responsibilities of the Legislative Yuan include passing laws, granting amnesty, making declarations of war or peace, and making resolutions about financial matters. Every bill must be passed in the Legislative Yuan and put into effect by the president.

The Judicial Yuan

The judicial branch of Taiwan's government has several levels of courts. A Constitutional Court reviews cases in which constitutional rights may have been violated. The Supreme Court, High Court, and District Courts handle civil and criminal trials. In Taiwan, there are no juries. Instead, judges decide all court cases.

Local Government

Taiwan has several levels of local governments. The region is divided into counties, each with its own government and council. The council makes county laws, and a magistrate serves as the county's chief official. A county magistrate super-

The Flag

The flag of the Republic of China features a red field with a dark blue rectangle in the upper-left corner. On the blue rectangle is a white sun with twelve triangle-shaped rays. The sun represents progress. Blue symbolizes liberty, justice, and democracy. Red is for brotherhood and sacrifice. White represents equality and honesty. The rays stand for the twelve months of the year and the twelve traditional Chinese hours.

vises the county as a whole. Larger cities within a county are usually run by an elected mayor.

Offshore islands also have governments. Penghu, Kinmen, and Lienchiang are considered counties because they have several cities and towns. Green Island, Orchid Island, and Pengjia Islet are smaller, but they also have magistrates.

Special municipalities are large cities that have city governments and councils responsible for laws and events dealing with their cities. There are five special municipalities: Taipei City, New Taipei City, Taichung, Tainan, and Kaohsiung. Mayors lead city councils, and voters elect the mayors for four-year terms. Mayors can serve only two terms in a row. Mayors choose two or three deputies to assist them, depending on the size of the city.

Hau Lung-pin is the mayor of Taipei, one of Taiwan's most important political positions. Each of the three most recent mayors of Taipei eventually became president of the Republic of China.

CHAPTER 6

A Global Economy

L I ZHI-PENG HAS SPENT THE LAST FIVE YEARS studying to become a digital design engineer. Digital designers draw the plans for building integrated circuit boards, the chips that run televisions, radios, cameras, cell phones, watches, and video game players. Taiwan is one of the world's major producers of integrated circuits. Engineers with Li Zhi-Peng's skills are in high demand.

The constant demand for faster, more powerful chips goes along with the constant upgrades in software, video games, smartphones, and portable computers. Taiwan is the world's leading producer of laptops, computer notebooks, and ultrabooks, and the components that they are made from.

Opposite: **A worker inspects computer chips at a factory.**

i-Taiwan 12 Projects

Since the early 2000s, Taiwan's economy has been on a financial roller coaster. The uncertainty of the economy caused problems for many political leaders. In the 2012 election, Taiwan president Ma Ying-jeou campaigned on ways to

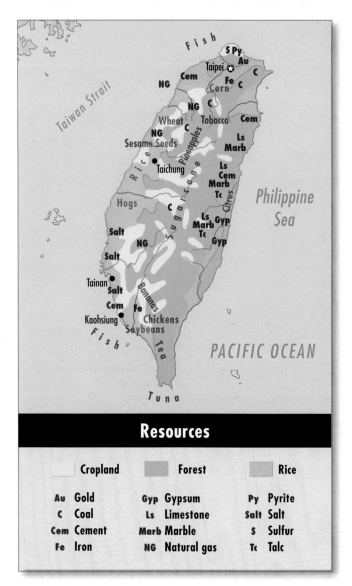

Resources

☐ Cropland	▨ Forest	▨ Rice

Au Gold	**Gyp** Gypsum	**Py** Pyrite
C Coal	**Ls** Limestone	**Salt** Salt
Cem Cement	**Marb** Marble	**S** Sulfur
Fe Iron	**NG** Natural gas	**Tc** Talc

improve the economy. The people of Taiwan wanted jobs, steady prices, affordable housing, and a solid, stable economy. Ma responded with the i-Taiwan 12 Projects program.

Much of this program deals with infrastructure—the roads, bridges, transportation, public buildings, ports, parks, and technology that keep a country running. First on the list of improvements is developing a faster, more convenient transportation network. The government plans to rebuild Kaohsiung port and the Taiwan Taoyuan International Airport. The blueprint also includes developing several industrial areas.

Environmental concerns also make up a significant part of the i-Taiwan 12 Projects. There is money to rebuild damaged coastal regions, prevent floods, and manage water. Planting trees and restoring forests will also support and improve the environment.

Agriculture

Before World War II, agriculture dominated Taiwan's economy. Since then, agriculture has represented an increasingly smaller piece of the economic pie. Rural farm life is not as appealing to Taiwan's youth as it once was. Industrial and service jobs pay better, and cities offer a wider variety of movies, restaurants, and recreation. Today, only 5 percent of Taiwanese workers are employed in agriculture.

One-quarter of the land that makes up Taiwan is used for farming, mostly in the west. While the country produces enough rice for its people, Taiwan must import wheat, corn, and soybeans, some of which are used for cattle feed.

A woman picks tea in the Ali Range. Oolong is the most common kind of tea grown in Taiwan.

The Beauty of Orchids

Taiwan's most stunning agricultural star is its orchid industry. Since the 1980s, orchids have been Taiwan's premier flower export. The worldwide orchid industry is worth US$2 billion annually, and Taiwan has a good portion of that business. Taiwan's rarest orchid varieties can bring more than US$1,000 per plant. The Taiwanese government is building the Taiwan Orchid Plantation, a controlled-atmosphere orchid farm featuring two hundred greenhouses. Nearly one-fourth of the world's orchids are grown in Taiwan's greenhouses, and Taiwan hopes to become the world's leading orchid supplier within the next few years.

Rice is the staple food of Taiwan. Everyone eats rice two or three times a day. By value, Taiwan's largest agricultural products are hogs, chickens, and rice. The top fruits grown include pineapples, mangoes, and betel nuts. Top vegetables include bamboo, cabbage, and shiitake mushrooms.

Raising livestock is the most profitable type of farming in Taiwan. Pig farmers produce hogs that become pork, ham, and bacon. Chickens are also common, and many households raise both chickens and ducks.

Taiwan's consumers have become used to a wide range of seafood products. Mullet are particularly popular for both their meat and eggs during the New Year's celebrations. Milkfish and tuna dominate the deep-sea fishing catches.

The Taiwanese fishing industry accounts for US$3.5 billion annually. Most of this production comes from deep-sea fisheries and inland aquaculture. Aquaculture is farming fish. Fish that

Colorful Koi

Stunningly beautiful koi swim in ornamental fishponds throughout the world. Among the most beautiful koi are those bred by Sing Chang Koi Farm. Company founder Chung Ying-ying began farming Taiwan koi after visiting Europe and learning that a fish-exporting business could be profitable. Koi is just one of the ornamental fish marketed by Taiwan to aquarium owners worldwide.

are farmed in Taiwan include grouper, cobia, shrimp, yellowtail tuna, sea bream, snappers, and tilapia. Taiwan also farms eels, a popular ingredient in both Chinese and Japanese food.

Workers adjust netting at a fish farm in Taiwan.

What Taiwan Grows, Makes, and Mines

AGRICULTURE (2010)

Hogs	7,068,621 animals
Rice	1,451,011 metric tons
Pineapples	420,172 metric tons

MANUFACTURING (2011)

Light-emitting diodes	34,814,863,000 units
Steel	22,878,525 metric tons
Integrated circuits	NT$1,562 billion in value added by manufacturing

MINING (2010)

Marble	25,118,000 metric tons
Cement	11,000,000 metric tons
Pig iron	9,358,000 metric tons

Mining

Taiwan has few natural resources and imports most of its coal, oil, and gas for energy production. In the past, sulfur, clay, and gold were mined in Taiwan. Today, marble and limestone are mined for building stone, crafts, and production of cement. Sand and gravel products are used in building and road construction.

Caustic soda, one of Taiwan's major mined minerals, is used to make paper, rayon, detergent, and other goods. Soda ash, another common Taiwan mineral, is used in making glass, pretzels, water softener, and grease removers. Taiwan also produces a great deal of lime, which is a basic ingredient in plaster, mortar for bricklaying, and whitewash.

Metal refineries process iron and steel. Steel is processed into billets, which are molds of freshly made steel in the form of metal bars or blocks. Steel bloom is the term for solid sections of steel cast from molten bars. Taiwan also refines nickel ore, which is used in making pots and pans, medical instruments, buildings, engines, coins, and batteries.

Factory Goods

Industry workers make products. A little more than one-third of all workers have jobs in industry. The electronics industry is the nation's largest employer. Although industrial workers do not grow food or catch fish, many work in food processing. They process food and package it for sale.

Textiles are among the many products made in Taiwan.

Taiwan uses the metric system for official measurement, but many Taiwanese rely on traditional units for everyday use.

Length

1 cun = 3.03 centimeters

1 chi = 10 cun = 30.3 cm

Area

1 ping = 3.3 square meters

1 mu = 30 ping = 99 sq m

1 jia = 2,934 ping = 9,699 sq m

1 li = 5 kah = 14,670 ping = 48,496 sq m

Volume of Bulk Goods

1 li = 37.5 milligrams

1 fen = 10 li = 375 mg

1 qian = 10 fen = 3.75 grams

1 liang = 10 qian = 37.5 g

1 jin = 16 liang = 600 g

1 dan = 100 jin = 60 kg

Taiwan's electronics industry churns out everything from light-emitting diodes (LEDs) and microchips to computers, cameras, cell phones and large-screen televisions. Electronic components also help run washing machines, refrigerators, electric fans, and automotive vehicles.

Fabrics, steel, and processed rubber made in Taiwan combine to make millions of the bicycles used in Taiwan. Other transportation products include engines and parts for cars, trucks, buses, and commercial vans. Taiwanese factories also produce car tires and automobile glass.

Services

Nearly 60 percent of people in Taiwan work in service industries. Service jobs include working in hotels and restaurants, banks and real estate companies, teaching, nursing, dental care, and child care. Such workers provide a service in return for pay.

Tourism is another important service industry in Taiwan. Service workers man the airports and harbors that welcome visitors to the island. Rental car agencies, taxis, and trains provide thousands of jobs supporting tourism. There are also hotel workers, restaurant workers, retail salespeople, and tour guides working in tourism.

Power Couple

Cher Wang (right) and Chen Wen-chi (below) are among the most prominent married couples in Taiwan. Wang is the co-founder and chairperson of HTC Corporation, a maker of smartphones, and of VIA Technologies, a maker of integrated chipsets. Her

husband, Chen Wen-chi, is president and CEO of VIA Technologies. The pair is worth US$8.8 billion, making them the wealthiest couple in Taiwan. In addition to their jobs in the electronics industry, the couple is heavily involved in charity work. They gave US$28.1 million to help found Guizhou Forerunner College in southwest China, and donated 6,000 HTC Flyer tablet PCs to sixty Taipei high schools.

The government is working to promote and support international tourism. One change that cost nothing was allowing individual tourists to come from China. Before 2011, Chinese tourists had to come as part of a group and remain with the group while in Taiwan. An increased number of airplane flights between China and Taiwan have brought a sea of tourists and Chinese business travelers to Taiwan.

Taiwan's Currency

Taiwan's currency is the New Taiwan Dollar, which uses the symbol NT$. Coins come in values of ½, 1, 5, 10, 20, and 50 New Taiwan dollars. Banknotes, or bills, come in values of 100, 200, 500, 1,000, and 2,000 New Taiwan dollars. They feature a variety of images from Taiwanese history and culture. For example, the 1,000 NT$ note depicts schoolchildren on the front of the bill and a pheasant and Mount Yu on the back. Each denomination is a different color. Both coins and bills increase in size as the value increases, and the value is printed in both Chinese characters and the Arabic numerals commonly used in the West. In 2013, 1 New Taiwan dollar equaled about 3 cents in U.S currency, and 1 U.S dollar equaled 30 New Taiwan dollars.

Getting Around Town

Taiwan's public transportation system is used heavily. It includes trains, light rail, and buses. Every day, nearly two million people take the Taipei metro system, which includes both subways and aboveground trains. Ridership on a high-speed rail system along the west coast of Taiwan has grown quickly since the route opened in 2007. The trains can reach speeds of 186 miles per hour (300 kpm).

Many people own cars, and motor scooters are a common way of getting around town. Biking is also popular. In Taipei, there are rental shops along the city's bike lanes, which are part of Taipei's YouBike bicycle-sharing system. The city is trying to reduce the car traffic and increase bike use as a "green" means of transportation. Taipei has 162 YouBike rental shops, and numbers have reached more than seven hundred thou-

How Much Does It Cost?

Cup of coffee	50 NT$	US$1.65
Bowl of noodles	90 NT$	US$3.00
Bus ride	15 NT$	US$0.50
Loaf of bread	80 NT$	US$2.70

sand rentals per month. Renters pick up a bike at one stop, pay a fee to use the bike for thirty minutes, and drop the bike off at the shop nearest their destination.

The streets of Taipei and other cities are packed with scooters. More than 60 percent of the population of Kaohsiung use scooters.

CHAPTER 7

In the City

TSENG HUA-CHU HAS LIVED ON A FARM ALL HIS LIFE. His parents and his grandparents have worked the same terraced rice paddy along the east coast of Taiwan for decades. The last crop is in, and Tseng Hua-chu bids farewell to his relatives. He is headed for Taipei to become a student at National Taiwan University.

Tseng Hua-chu has found an apartment in Taipei that he will share with a friend. The apartment is small, but it has two bedrooms and is already furnished. The university is in the Da-An district, one of the most expensive areas of Taipei and beyond their budget, so they will live in Haishan. It is three blocks from the metro line, which will provide a quick trip into the city.

The young man's leaving is bittersweet for his family. The Tsengs have lived south of Hualien for eighty years. Like so many of Taiwan's youth, Tseng Hua-chu's future is in the city, and his parents will not be passing their land on to him.

Opposite: **Shoppers fill a narrow street in Jiufen. Taiwan has the second-highest population density in the world among countries with a population of at least ten million.**

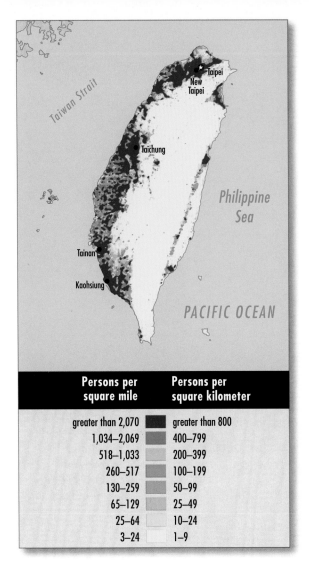

Persons per square mile		Persons per square kilometer
greater than 2,070		greater than 800
1,034–2,069		400–799
518–1,033		200–399
260–517		100–199
130–259		50–99
65–129		25–49
25–64		10–24
3–24		1–9

Population of Major Cities (2012 est.)

City	Population
New Taipei	3,913,595
Kaohsiung	2,773,885
Taichung	2,662,770
Taipei	2,647,122
Tainan	1,876,706

Growing Cities

Most of Taiwan's people live on about one-third of the island's land. One city runs into the next along the western coast and in the north. A few smaller cities lie along the eastern coastline, but few people live in the nation's mountainous center. The coastal regions have abundant jobs, schools, hospitals, and shopping opportunities.

In 2013, Taiwan had an estimated population of 23,299,716. About three-quarters of the population live in cities, and the cities are becoming larger and more densely packed as more and more people move there from the countryside. Taiwanese cities are growing at a rate of 4 percent each year, while the overall population is only growing at 0.27 percent yearly.

Ethnic Taiwan

Most people in Taiwan—84 percent—are Taiwanese. They are descended from people who moved from mainland China to Taiwan between the 1600s and the early 1900s. Mainland Chinese people make up another 14 percent of the population. They are people who moved from mainland China to Taiwan after 1945. The remaining 2 percent of the people in Taiwan are aborigines.

The government recognizes fourteen aborigine groups. Aborigines have suffered discrimination since the arrival of Chinese and Japanese on the island. Even today, while aborigines have better living conditions and legally protected rights, most remain at the bottom of the economic scale in Taiwan. In 1984, native people formed the Alliance of Taiwan Aborigines to promote fairness and equality for all aborigines. A cabinet-level post, the Council of Indigenous Peoples, was added to the Executive Yuan in 1996. More recently, a twenty-four-hour cable station, the Indigenous Television Network, went on the air to promote aboriginal languages, report aboriginal news, and provide aboriginal entertainment.

Ethnic Taiwan (2012)	
Taiwanese	84%
Mainland Chinese	14%
Aborigines	2%

Taiwanese aborigines demonstrate in front of government offices. Taiwanese aborigines have become more politically active in recent years.

Aborigine Cultures

Like other people in Taiwan, Taiwanese aborigines go to work and school. They wear jeans and ride scooters and play video games. Although they are fully a part of modern Taiwan, they also belong to distinct cultures, and some work to maintain their traditional ways.

The fourteen official Taiwan aborigine groups are the Ami, Atayal, Bunun, Kavalan, Paiwan, Puyuma, Rukai, Saisiyat, Sakizaya, Sediq, Tao, Thao, Truku, and Tsou. Official government recognition brings benefits to the people in the form of government money for schools, hospitals, libraries, and other community projects. Many aborigines live in the Central Mountain region or along the eastern coastline.

The Ami are Taiwan's largest aborigine group, with 170,000 people. Many Ami live in the city of Taitung, on the east coast, but there are also small Ami villages along the coast and in the valley to the west.

The Atayal live in the mountains of northern Taiwan. With a population of about 81,000, they are the second-largest aborigine group. The Atayal strongly reject becoming part of the Chinese-based culture of Taiwan.

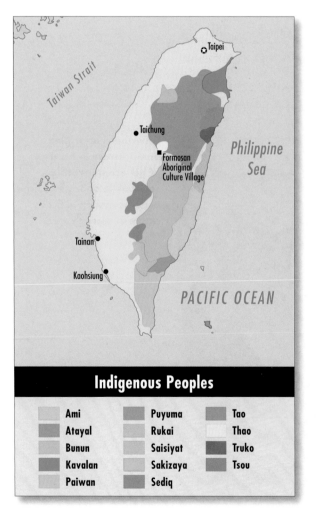

Indigenous Peoples

Ami
Atayal
Bunun
Kavalan
Paiwan
Puyuma
Rukai
Saisiyat
Sakizaya
Sediq
Tao
Thao
Truko
Tsou

The Bunun live in the Central Mountain area in small, remote villages. Each year, the Bunun hold the Ear-Shooting Festival, a coming-of-age ceremony in which Bunun hunters show their archery skill. The Bunun staple food is millet, a grain grown on mountain plateaus and slopes. Popular singer Wang Hong-en and novelist Topas Tamapima are Bunun.

The Paiwan people occupy parts of Pingtung and Taitung counties in southern Taiwan. In Kenting National Park,

An Atayal man in traditional dress

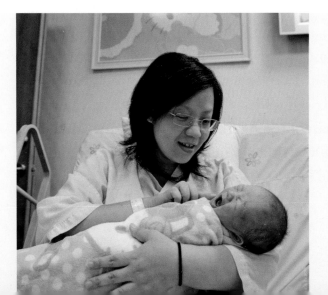

What's in a Name?

Choosing the right name for a child is serious business. Most Taiwanese parents choose two-character names. Most male names indicate virtues of strength, ability, or power. Female names often refer to characteristics of beauty, grace, or charm. In southern Taiwan, nicknames are formed by adding A- to the name, such as A-mei, who is a popular singer.

Tao men arrive in Tamsui, near Taipei, after paddling their boat about 370 miles (600 km) from their home on Orchid Island.

many Paiwan people live in traditional homes made of stone slabs. The Paiwan honor the hundred-pacer snake, which is depicted often in Paiwan art, clothing, and jewelry. The snake is believed to protect the Paiwan people and maintain peace between them and other aborigines.

There are about 3,500 Tao people in Taiwan today. They live on Orchid Island, and their remoteness from everyday Taiwanese life has helped them retain their traditions. The people live in huts made of woven straw and reeds. The Tao carve totems to protect their people from evil spirits. A seafaring tribe, the Tao celebrate their fishing culture each year with the launching of a new boat. Fishing vessels are made from one large tree that has been carved out and decorated.

Taiwanese aborigines have lost many of their traditions. Traditional facial tattooing has lost popularity, and most aborigines follow Christianity instead of their traditional religions. Aboriginal languages continue to be spoken, supported

With tender care

Let us set in motion

> our blood that is once again warm

Let us recall

> our songs

> our dances

> our sacred rituals

And the tradition

> of unselfish mutual coexistence

Between us and the earth

by aboriginal studies in Taiwan's schools and the Indigenous Television Network. It is in part through television that aboriginal cultures keep their native tongues alive.

The Atayal people traditionally got facial tattoos as part of a coming-of-age ritual, but now the practice has almost entirely died out.

The Chinese Language

The people of Taiwan speak Mandarin Chinese and Taiwanese. Many also speak English and Japanese. Mandarin is Taiwan's official language. Chinese is a character-based language rather than an alphabet-based language. Each character represents a syllable of the spoken language. Some characters represent whole words, but many words are formed by combining characters. There are tens of thousands of characters, but most people memorize and practice only a few thousand. Compared to learning the twenty-six letters of the English language, reading and writing Mandarin is difficult.

In the People's Republic of China, characters have been simplified to make them easier to read and write. Taiwan continues to use traditional Chinese characters.

Chinese has many dialects, or versions, of which Mandarin is the most common. Many people in Taiwan also speak Taiwanese, a version of the Minnan dialect from the Fujian region of China. Seven out of ten people in Taiwan speak this language.

Going to School

Taiwan has one of the best-educated populations in the world. For many people in Taiwan, schooling begins with two years of pre-school. This is followed by six years of primary school, three years of junior high school, and another three years in high school.

Elementary school students in Taiwan have a long day compared to children in the United States. The school day begins at 7:30 a.m. and ends at 5:00 p.m. In addition to schoolwork, students are responsible for cleaning the school, as schools do not hire janitors to clean up. Classes are taught in Mandarin Chinese, and studying English is available from the third grade.

A Taiwanese boy adjusts a model of a wind turbine at a robot competition. Elementary school children study subjects such as math, science, social studies, music, and art.

Taiwan's government supports several different types of high schools. Ordinary and comprehensive high schools prepare students to go to college. Magnet high schools focus on specific topics, such as technology, math, music, or art. There are also experimental senior high schools, such as a school that is bilingual. Vocational schools teach industry-related subjects, such as welding, auto repair, or agriculture. Most schools in Taiwan offer English classes in addition to language arts, math, science, and history.

A typical high school in Taiwan has eight classes a day, five or six days a week. Students have to take a nap for thirty minutes after lunch, and tests are given most days. Students attend two semesters of twenty weeks each, but they are expected to study during the summer and winter breaks.

After school ends at 5:00, many students head to cram classes. The cram classes are to help the students pass the yearly tests given in math, language, and other subjects. Cram class runs from 6:00 p.m. to 9:30 p.m., and then it is time to head home and do homework.

Taiwan has more than one hundred colleges and universities. The largest is National Taiwan University in Taipei, which has nearly eighteen thousand undergraduate students and another twelve thousand graduate students doing more advanced studies.

College students head to class in Taichung. About 39 percent of Taiwanese adults have a college education.

CHAPTER 8

Religion and Respect

IT IS THE FIFTH DAY OF THE FIFTH MONTH IN THE Chinese calendar. Today begins the Dragon Boat Festival, honoring the life of the great Chinese scholar and poet Qu Yuan. Families get together to share rice dumplings and hang herbs around the home. Some people wear herbs that are said to chase away disease. It is also said that if a person balances an egg on its end at high noon on this day, Double Fifth Day, the rest of his or her year will be filled with luck and good health.

The people of Taiwan practice several different religions, and philosophies, including Confucianism, Taoism, folk religion, Buddhism, Christianity, and Taiwan aborigine religions. Many people practice more than one religion. For example, it is common for people to mix elements of Taoism and Buddhism.

Opposite: **A family prays at a Buddhist temple in Tainan.**

Boys dance at a ceremony honoring the birthday of Confucius.

Confucianism and Taoism are native to China, while Buddhism originated in India, and Christianity came to the island through Western missionaries. Aborigine beliefs arose with the native people of Taiwan, although many of them now practice other religions as well.

Confucianism

Some people consider Confucianism a religion, but others say it is more of a philosophy because it is not concerned with gods or life after death. Confucianism follows the teachings of Kongzi (551–479 BCE), known in the West as Confucius. He believed that if people were morally good and honest, society would be happy. Confucius is sometimes remembered for teaching his ideas through sayings, such as "To know what you know and know what you do not know—this then is wisdom."

Religion in Taiwan	
Mixture of Buddhist and Taoist	93%
Christian	4.5%
Other	2.5%

Taoism

Taoism, based on the teachings of Laozi, who is said to have lived in the sixth century BCE, encourages followers to live in harmony with the world. Leading a good life means replacing personal greed with naturalness and simplicity. Taoism is linked to practices such as *feng shui* and the belief in *yin* and *yang*. Feng shui, literally "wind and water," is a way of balancing energy to make sure a person has good luck and health. Yin and yang are opposite principles that complement each other. One cannot exist without the other. Examples of yin and yang are cold and hot, and dark and light.

A man lights incense at a Taoist temple dedicated to Guan Gong, the god of war.

Major Taoist festivals held in Taiwan include the Jade Emperor's birthday, the Queen Mother of the West's birthday, and the Supreme Emperor of the Dark Heaven's birthday. Taoists believe the Jade Emperor is the leader of the heavenly gods. Ceremonies take place annually in temples in Daxi, Taichung, and Tainan. The Queen Mother of the West's events are mainly held in Hualien. She is the highest-ranking female god and is usually depicted as the Jade Emperor's wife. The Supreme Emperor is believed to control the elements. There are four hundred temples dedicated to this god, whose greatest power is over fire.

A man dressed as a Taoist god parades through the streets of Taipei during a festival.

The Legend of Mazu

Lin Mo-niang was born in Fujian province around 960 CE. Her father and brother were fishermen. Lin Mo-niang is said to have had the ability to predict storms at sea, shipwrecks, and other disasters. According to legend, she tried to save her father and brother when their ship got caught in a storm. But despite her efforts, they disappeared into the sea. Since then, it is believed her spirit protects people traveling the sea from danger. The people of her village built the first temple in her honor in about 990, and the goddess Mazu has been worshipped ever since.

Folk Religion

Taiwan has a vibrant folk religion tradition filled with many deities. Some of these deities began as ordinary people who became heroes, and then were raised up to the level of gods after they died. The goddess Mazu is such a deity. She is the guardian of sailors and fishers. There are many temples to Mazu, and many people who follow Mazu take part in an annual pilgrimage between Dajia and Xingang in her honor.

Buddhism

Taiwan is a major center for Buddhism. The two forms of Buddhism most often practiced in Taiwan are Pure Land and Zen Buddhism. Pure Land Buddhism depends on chanting to help achieve a level of enlightenment or happiness. Zen Buddhism relies on meditation, which is deep thought about the path to happiness.

The Buddha

The person who became known as Buddha was born Siddhartha Gautama in India about 563 BCE. Gautama came from a wealthy family. At age twenty-nine, he left his privileged life to live simply, meditate, and try to understand human suffering. Finally, after several years, he came to realize that suffering ends when desires are overcome. By giving up the desire for money, power, and worldly goods, Gautama explained, one can achieve inner peace, or nirvana. Gautama became known as the Buddha, "the Enlightened One." He spent the remaining decades of his life spreading his teachings. He died in about 483 BCE.

One of the biggest events in the Buddhist calendar for the people of Taiwan is Buddha's birthday. According to legend, on the day Buddha was born, a heavenly dragon washed him in streams of scented water. In Taiwan, worshippers conduct the Bathing the Buddha Ceremony. They make offerings of flowers, fruits, and tea. They light candles, and set up a bathing site near the temple to bathe the statue of the young Buddha. This is a time to rid oneself of greed and selfishness, do kind and generous deeds, and think about the path to enlightenment.

Aboriginal Ceremonies

Traditionally, each Taiwanese aborigine group had its own religion. Each religion included the belief in a variety of spirits and in the power of sacred symbols. The Chinese who immigrated to the island brought Taoist and Buddhist beliefs, which, over time, were incorporated into aborigine religious practice. Today, the majority of Taiwanese aborigines are Christian.

Many Taiwan aborigines still take part in the traditional religious festivals that fill the year with singing, dancing, and feasting. Many others keep their religious celebrations private. They do not encourage visitors though they do allow small groups of travelers to take part in harvest festivals, which are less religious and more community oriented. Celebrations may change dates at the last minute if a tribal elder feels that signs point to a different day being better for the festival.

Tsou people take part in a ceremony dedicated to their god of war.

In February, the Tsou honor their warrior traditions in the Mayasvi Festival. They give thanks to the god of war and the god of heaven for warriors' victories through feasting and dance. Later in the year, the Bunun and the Puyuma hold ear-shooting festivals. Hunting the ears of large deer represents having a good hunt during the year. This is a coming-of-age festival when boys are welcomed into the tribe as men.

A family shrine in Tainan. At these shrines, people burn incense and make offerings.

Up in Smoke

Burning ghost money to honor ancestors has become a fire hazard, as Taiwanese people go through 100,000 to 250,000 tons (90,000 to 225,000 metric tons) of ghost money every year. This has led the government to recommend burning ghost credit cards or ghost checks that cover large amounts of money, in order to reduce fire hazards. In Taipei, a local company offers an online service to allow citizens to respect their ancestors through a combined paper-burning event.

Respect for Ancestors

The people of Taiwan have great respect for their ancestors. They honor the spirits of the dead in several ways. Most Taiwanese families have shrines in their homes, where they make offerings to their ancestors or favorite deities.

Taiwanese people also show respect to their ancestors during Ghost Month, which is part of the folk religion. This time of year includes feasting at huge banquets, lighting altars, and burning spirit paper money. It is said that ghosts haunt the island throughout the month, and every effort is made to keep the ghosts happy. It is also said that spirits need funds for traveling to the afterworld, and spirit paper money (often gold in color) is burned to give the spirits more money for their trips. Late at night, boats glide out of local harbors to release lanterns on the ocean.

Taiwan also celebrates the Pure Bright Festival, or Tomb Sweeping Day. Held in the spring, this day finds people traveling to tombs and cemeteries to pay visits to the spirits of their ancestors. Families sweep away dead grass from the gravesites and burn ghost money.

CHAPTER 9

Music, Movies, and Martial Arts

TAIWAN HAS A RICH CULTURAL HERITAGE, FROM OPERA to hip-hop, literature to graphic novels, movies to martial arts. The traditional arts of ceramics, bronzes, and calligraphy link Taiwan to China and Japan. Wood carving, stonework, and weaving connect modern Taiwan to its aboriginal origins. Today's popular arts—music, movies, and martial arts—blend East and West to create a flavor that is uniquely Taiwanese.

Opposite: **In classical Chinese opera, the performers often wear elaborate costumes and makeup.**

Music

Western classical music is popular in Taiwan. Symphony orchestras from around the world perform concerts there, and many Taiwanese children study violin, piano, or other instruments.

Another type of classical music in Taiwan is the Chinese opera. This includes traditional Chinese instruments and singing styles. But Chinese opera is much more than music. Colorful costumes swirl, artists perform somersaults and backflips, and actors pantomime classic roles.

The Taiwanese version of Chinese opera is usually an outdoor event. It is common to see opera presented in a marketplace, a neighborhood park, or the front courtyard

Mandopop

Singers from Taiwan and Hong Kong have made an impact on the radio with their own version of pop music. Broken hearts, teen tragedies, and lost loves provide the themes for top performers. The songs, sung in Mandarin Chinese, form the basis of mandopop. Handsome singers and polished videos help propel mandopop songs to the top of the charts. Among the popular mandopop artists are A-mei (right), Sarah Chen, and Blacklist Studio.

of a temple. Taiwan's classic opera has four main characters. They appear in puppet theater, minor opera, and great opera. Chou, the clown, always appears with a white patch on his nose. Chou actors play ugly, nasty characters and are usually male. Jing, the painted-face character, is sometimes evil and occasionally sly—but always male. Dan is the female lead and wears white and red face makeup. Dan female roles may be old crones, sweet young ladies, or doting wives and mothers. Dan's counterpart is Sheng, the main male character. Only the most skilled actors are cast as Sheng.

Puppet theater blends music and imagination. Taiwan has three types of puppet theater: shadow puppets, glove puppets, and giant puppets. For *piying xi*, shadow puppet theater, the puppet figures appear as shadows against a screen. The audience watches the shadows dance, telling age-old stories. *Budaixi*, glove puppet theater, takes place in a small, boxlike stage. The puppeteers handle bells, gongs, drums, and perform martial arts moves as they turn and twist the puppets onstage. *Kuilei xi*, giant puppet theater, mainly uses marionettes, which are large puppets on strings. Puppet theater began as entertainment at religious festivals and is still popular on television and at public events.

The Arts

Classical Taiwanese arts include calligraphy, bronze work, ceramics, and cloisonné. Calligraphy is the fine art of handwriting. Done with a brush and ink, calligraphy was highly prized and rewarded in ancient Chinese courts. A skilled calligrapher needs a steady hand—there are no erasers for fixing mistakes. The National Palace Museum in Taipei displays excellent examples of calligraphy from as early as the eleventh century.

King of Puppet Theater

Huang Hai-tai (1901–2007) spent ninety years performing in Taiwanese puppet theater. He taught several hundred pupils how to handle glove puppets. Huang wrote his own scripts, many of which he based on popular novels. He continued performing until he reached the age of one hundred. His talent lives on through his many students who continue presenting glove puppet theater in Huang's style.

Master Sculptor

The Ju Ming Museum focuses on the artistry of sculptor Ju Ming (1938-). Ju Ming is known for his modern metal or wood sculptures, as well as realistic carvings of people in ordinary settings. His *Men with Umbrellas* looks like a group of men waiting in the rain for a train to arrive. The museum features an entertaining sculpture of Albert Einstein and several modern views of the system of exercise called tai chi.

Bronze work is seen on relics from more than three thousand years ago. Examples include bowls inlaid with turquoise, statues of fierce beasts, musical instruments, and weapons. Bronzes are also found in temples. Bronze is used in incense burners, carved dragon columns, and large, beautifully worked doors.

Taiwanese children take part in a pottery class. The art of ceramics continues to thrive in Taiwan today.

The National Palace Museum

Anyone who wants to see the world's largest collection of Chinese artifacts should head to Taiwan's National Palace Museum. The building houses seven hundred thousand items, although only fifteen thousand are displayed at any one time.

Most of the works were originally collected by the Chinese imperial family. In the 1930s, when the Japanese were about to invade China, the collection was put into storage and moved south for safekeeping. Then, in 1949, as the Nationalists fled China for Taiwan, they took part of the collection with them.

Long-term exhibits include bronzes, calligraphy, carved jade, and pottery. Rare books, priceless ceramics, and stunning bronzes have permanent exhibitions. The museum also houses classic Chinese paintings of ink and color on silk and paper. Most of these paintings are scrolls that feature mountain scenes or landscapes. Among the museum's treasures are *Early Spring* by Kou Shi Hang and *Travelers Amid Mountains and Streams* by Fan Kuan.

Ceramics is the art of pottery. It ranges from the delicate, nearly see-through vases crafted in the kilns of ancient Chinese courts to the practical bowls made by Taiwanese aborigines. Some of the most remarkable Taiwanese pots are the simplest. They are cord-marked, hand-painted pots that are hardened in open fires.

Cloisonné is an art form that balances metalwork and enamels. Thin wires of silver or gold outline a decorative pattern. Each tiny space is filled with colorful enamel and then fired to set the design. Large cloisonné pieces include plates, figurines, and incense burners. Small pieces may be rings, earrings, or necklaces.

Shoppers browse at a bookstore in Taipei. As in the United States, many bookstores in Taiwan have closed because more and more people shop online or read e-books.

Literature

In Taiwan, authors have not always been able to express their thoughts freely. When the country was under Japanese control, some of the literature being produced reflected the oppression of a colonized people. In 1945, Wu Zhuoliu completed *Orphan of Asia*, a novel that parallels Taiwan's coming into being. *Orphan of Asia* is often read in Taiwan literature classes. Under Chiang Kai-shek's rule, literature from the People's Republic of China was kept out of Taiwan. Taiwanese writers developed their own style of work, careful not to offend the nation's ruling party.

Today, Taiwan has a lively literary scene. Some works cut through the false face of politics while others describe the reality of aboriginal life. The works may be dry and harsh, or romantic, funny, or sad. Western books, particularly ones that are made into movies, fly off bookstore shelves. Two Taiwanese books that became popular television shows are *Big Hospital Small Doctor* by Hou Wun-yong and *The Hooligan Professor* by Lin Jian-long.

Graphic novels are growing in popularity in Taiwan. A large volume of material from Korea and Japan floods Taiwan's bookstores. As a result, many graphic novelists belong to the Taipei City Comic Artists Guild, which helps promote local artists and their work. Graphic novels attract readers of all ages, and Ko Ming-wa's *Lovely, Lovely, Lovely!* and Shen Ying-jie's *The Bai Hua Café* have both won awards in the Taiwan comic artists' community. Taiwan hopes to become a major provider of quality graphic novels.

Young people read at a comic book fair in Taipei. Japanese comics, or manga, are extremely popular in Taiwan.

Movies and Martial Arts

Taiwan's movie industry has been active since the early days of movie history. When the nation's movie industry began in 1901, the Japanese government controlled the movies that were made. After the war, the KMT maintained a strong hand on the content of new films. By the 1980s, most of the movies made in Taiwan were martial arts action flicks. Dozens of martial artists stepped into acting roles and became instant stars.

Martial arts attract many athletes in Taiwan. Taiwan has masters of judo, jujitsu, aikido, tae kwon do, and tai chi. Several of the most gifted martial artists began appearing in

Angela Mao attacks three men at once in a scene from the 1972 film *Hapkido*.

movies, showcasing their strength, speed, and skill. Among these artists are Chiang Sheng, who appeared in *Five Deadly Venoms*; Cynthia Khan, from *In the Line of Duty 3*; and Angela Mao, nicknamed Lady Whirlwind. Mao appeared in the martial arts classic *Enter the Dragon*.

The 1980s brought a style of filmmaking called the New Wave. Films became more realistic and mirrored Taiwanese life instead of promoting government issues or martial arts. Leading members of Taiwan's New Wave include Hou Hsiao-hsien, director of such films as *A City of Sadness* and *The Puppetmaster*; and Edward Yang, director of *Yi Yi* and *A Confucian Confusion*. In the years since New Wave began, Taiwan's film industry has blossomed.

Director Ang Lee shot much of his 2012 film *Life of Pi* in Taiwan. Based on the book by Yann Martel, it is the story of a young man stranded on a boat with a Bengal tiger. Lee won an Oscar for his work on the visually unique *Life of Pi*, and the

Number One with the Clubs

Yani Tseng is a world-class women's golf pro. She became number one in the world in 2011, when, at age twenty-two, she became the youngest player, male or female, to win five major championships. By 2013, she had twenty-six titles to her name.

Many Taiwanese start their day with tai chi. It is a form of exercise that uses slow movements and emphasizes a calm state of mind.

movie has given a serious boost to Taiwan's production companies. Taiwan's movie industry turns out fifteen to twenty films each year. The companies produce romantic comedies, thrillers, action adventures, and serious dramas.

Movie theaters are packed on the weekends, and films made in Taiwan are shown along with movies from China and Hong Kong. Theaters also show American and British movies, most of which are dubbed in Mandarin Chinese. Taiwanese people also enjoy watching on their large-screen TVs movies that Taiwan produces for its citizens and for export.

Sports

Although most Taiwanese people feel that regular exercise is ideal for good health, finding time for such activity is not easy. Many people get their exercise by riding bikes to and from school or work. Others jog after work, prac-

tice yoga, dance, play badminton, or go swimming. Mountain hiking is a great way to spend a weekend, and many families head for the hills to go camping.

Baseball is the most popular team sport in Taiwan. There are teams at all age and ability levels, from elementary school through professional leagues. Aborigines make up a large proportion of the top pro ball players in Taiwan. Many of these players come from Hualien and Taitung counties. Many Americans also play on professional baseball teams in Taiwan.

Today, Japanese and United States professional ball teams court Taiwan's top players. Guo Yuan-zhi and Kuo Tai-yuan, two superstars in Japan, got their start on Taiwan's Little League teams. Chin-Feng Chen, Chin-lung Hu, and Hong-Chih Kuo have played for the Los Angeles Dodgers, while Chien-Ming Wang has pitched for the New York Yankees and the Washington Nationals.

Basketball is growing in popularity. There are hoops in all public playgrounds, and the only thing players need for a pick-up game is a ball.

CHAPTER 10

All in the Family

HUANG FEI-YEN AND LIN SHENG ARE EXPECTING their first child within the next few weeks. The birth will follow the Taiwanese practice of *zuoyuezi*, which means "sitting out a month." Modern Taiwanese birth recovery centers combine old ways with the new. A center is sometimes more like a hotel than a hospital, with a swimming pool, gym, and Jacuzzi spa. The mother, the father, and the baby will stay there for up to a month.

By Chinese tradition, new mothers must rest to recover from a birth. Mothers-in-law used to provide a month of constant care for mother and child. New mothers were not supposed to exercise, wash their hair, or go outside. Doctors have found that sitting out a month to recover is good for new mothers, although exercise is now encouraged. The new birth centers replace mothers-in-law with exercise coaches, Chinese medicine healers, and trained chefs to support the new moms.

Opposite: **A Taiwanese family enjoys a walk in the park. Taiwan has one of the world's lowest birthrates, with the average woman having only one child.**

Marriage

Some marriages in Taiwan follow old Chinese traditions and some are thoroughly modern. More often, however, Taiwanese couples have weddings that combine the old and the new. Traditionally, a matchmaker introduces the couple, although this seldom happens today. If the match works out, an engagement ceremony and a wedding follow. The bride and groom wear red, the Chinese color for good luck.

A formal engagement has two parts—the tea ceremony and the ring ceremony. Both are held at the bride's house. At the tea ceremony, the bride offers the groom and his family cups of sweet tea. When they have finished, she collects the cups. The groom and his relatives put red envelopes with money into an empty teacup. The envelopes symbolize a dowry, a payment made to the family of the bride.

The Taiwanese tea ceremony uses small cups and requires careful attention to the temperature of the water and the amount of tea.

In the ring ceremony, the bride and groom exchange rings. It is bad luck for a ring to slip to the base of the finger, so the bride and groom both bend their fingers to keep the rings on the end. After the engagement ceremony, the groom burns incense for his ancestors.

For the wedding, the groom and his relatives go to the bride's home to honor her ancestors by burning sticks of incense. As the groom arrives, the bride's family offers trays of tangerines, sunflower seeds, or candy. Friends of the bride then request promises from the groom, and he offers a red envelope with NT$999 or another amount that uses only nines to guarantee lasting love. Soon, the bride and groom leave the bride's home. Because it is said that no sun should shine on the bride's head, a rice sieve or black umbrella shades her from the sun. Sugarcane is tied to the car's roof to bring sweetness to the marriage.

Grooms hold umbrellas over their brides' heads at a group wedding in Taiwan.

Say Cheese!

No Taiwanese wedding is complete without three important people—the bride, the groom, and the wedding photographer. Nearly a year before their wedding, couples book their wedding photographer. Some time before the wedding, the bride dons a stunning wedding dress, while the groom wears a tuxedo. Couples pose by the sea, in fields of wildflowers, or in a national park. Even quaint street markets provide backgrounds for a happy couple's wedding photographs. Taiwanese wedding photography is so popular that couples come to Taiwan from all over Asia to commemorate their wedding days.

The couple returns to the groom's house, where the bride and groom take part in ceremonies to get rid of any evil. This usually involves firecrackers. Inside the home, another tea ceremony is held, and the bride is recognized as a member of the groom's family.

For a modern wedding, the bride often enters the wedding banquet three times wearing three different wedding dresses. The bride usually wears a Western-style white gown, a pastel gown, and a traditional Chinese gown.

Many couples hold their wedding ceremonies in a restaurant or hotel. It is common for the guests to enjoy a twelve-course dinner. Every guest gives the couple a red envelope with money in it, and, in return, the couple gives each guest wedding cookies. This lavish banquet features many toasts and speeches that honor the bride, groom, or family. It is the center of the public part of the marriage ceremony.

Whether traditional or modern, the important part of a wedding is starting the bride and groom off well in their new life together. Both families hope for a successful marriage and for children.

Some funerals in Taiwan include attendants dressed as large masked figures.

Funeral Rites

Taiwan's large Buddhist population believes in reincarnation—that after death the soul is reborn. A person's fate in the next life is determined by the way he or she lived in this life, and the person's good deeds. Buddhists also believe that praying and making offerings improve what happens to a soul after death.

Few Taiwanese Buddhists die in hospitals. When death is near, the person is taken home and put to bed to die. Upon death, the body remains in the bed for ten hours so that the soul can easily pass on to a happy place. Seven days of mourning follow a death, and relatives and friends honor the dead by giving the family white envelopes filled with money. White is the color of mourning and sadness in Taiwan.

Whether Buddhist, Taoist, or Christian, most Taiwanese deceased are cremated. Ashes are placed in urns and put in family tombs. Buddhist families go to a temple and chant weekly for seven weeks. Taoists burn ghost money to honor their dead. They believe the money will make for an easier journey to the afterlife. Funerals are colorful and lively. There are tables filled with food to feed the mourners. Families hire brass bands, dancers, and professional mourners.

Holidays

Holidays are family time in Taiwan. The year begins with Founding Day, which marks the day Sun Yat-sen founded the Provisional Government of the Republic of China in 1912. In January or February, families celebrate the Chinese New Year with fireworks, parades, and feasting. Giving money in red envelopes or decorating windows and doors with red guarantees good luck throughout the coming year.

Taiwan's Professional Mourners

Liu Jun-lin has cried her way to the top of her profession. She is Taiwan's most famous professional mourner, and her services are in high demand. At funerals, she puts on a white robe and hood and crawls to the coffin on her hands and knees sobbing loudly. "Every funeral you go to, you have to feel this family is your own family," Liu says. "When I see so many people grieving, I get even sadder."

The tradition of professional mourners started when young women left home to work and could not return in time for a family funeral. The family hired a "replacement daughter" to provide an appropriate level of sorrow.

National Holidays

January 1	Founding Day
January/February	Chinese New Year
February 28	228 Memorial Day
April 4	Children's Day
April 4 or 5	Tomb Sweeping Day
May 1	Labor Day
May or June	Dragon Boat Festival
September or October	Mid-Autumn Festival
October 10	National Day/Double Ten Day

Several holidays celebrate family connections. On 228 Memorial Day, flags are flown at half-mast to show respect for the dead. This holiday recalls thousands of protesters who were killed by government forces beginning on February 28, 1947. Families attend memorial services and concerts to

Taiwanese students perform at a National Day celebration.

honor those who died. The Children's Day holiday reminds people of the rights of children and promotes efforts to stop child abuse. Tomb Sweeping Day is a day for family picnics and honoring ancestors. In September or October, the Mid-Autumn Festival is celebrated with family reunions.

What's to Eat?

Breakfast and dinner are daily family events in Taiwan. Both Japanese and Chinese cooking heavily influence Taiwanese food. Visitors to Taiwan often find that the combination of these cooking styles provides some of the best eating in Asia.

Paper lanterns are released into the air at the Lantern Festival, at the end of Chinese New Year.

Musical Garbage Trucks

Not too long ago, Taiwan had a major garbage problem. The country's large population put their trash by the side of the street, attracting rats and other scavengers. The government came up with a unique solution—musical garbage trucks. The trucks play music, much like ice cream trucks, and city-dwellers come out of their homes and put their garbage directly into the trucks. Most trucks play the music of German composer Ludwig van Beethoven throughout the year and Chinese music for Chinese New Year.

Breakfast for a Taiwanese family is often based on leftovers. Whatever was last night's dinner becomes today's breakfast. When there are no leftovers, breakfast is *congee, you tiao,* and *doujiang.* Congee is rice cereal. You tiao is deep-fried dough, like a crunchy doughnut, that is dipped in congee. Doujiang is slightly sweet soybean milk, served cold in the summer and warm in the winter.

Taiwanese people add several small dishes to round out a typical congee breakfast. Common condiments include peanuts, dried radish, fresh vegetables, and pickled cabbage or cucumber. Some people add preserved duck eggs, *xian ya dan,* which have orange-red yolks. Egg sandwiches are also a popular breakfast food.

Breakfast from a street vendor or a bakery includes steamed buns (with or without meat or vegetable filling) and *jianbing* or *danbing,* a crepe-like pancake filled with meat or egg. Shops also offer *shaobing* (a soft flatbread like pita) and *guotie* (fried dumplings). Most Taiwanese breakfast foods are savory or salty rather than sweet.

Lunch may be any cuisine, and it is usually eaten at school, in restaurants, or from street carts. The most popular lunch is noodle soup. Another popular take-out option is *biandang,* a boxed lunch with several compartments filled with different

Diners enjoy steaming bowls of food at a restaurant in Taipei.

foods. The basic food is steamed rice. The rest of the meal includes meat or fish, eggs, dried bean curd, vegetables, sauce, and sliced pickled ginger.

Taiwan has a number of cafeteria-style self-service restaurants. Some are vegetarian, while others offer pork, chicken, and fish in addition to vegetables. Diners fill up their trays with what they want and pay by the weight. Called *zizhu canting*, self-serve shops are usually open for both lunch and dinner.

The people of Taiwan eat dinner fairly early. This is particularly true for families with school-aged children. Junior high and high school students often go to cram school from 6:00 to 9:30 p.m., so an early dinner is essential. A popular winter food is *huo guo*, or hot pot. Huo guo literally means "fire pot." The dish starts with a pot of simmering chicken, pork, or vegetable stock. A plate of ingredients (meat, shrimp, fish, eggs, and vegetables) is placed on the table to be cooked during the meal. This method of cooking and lively conversation keep the diners warm on cold Taiwanese winter nights.

Night markets offer late-night snacks for people out on the town. These snacks are the Taiwanese version of fast food. Each market has a specialty. Noodle soups include *niurou mian*, made with beef, and *danzi mian*, made with pork. Changhua city's signature dish is pork meatballs with mushrooms and bamboo shoots that are wrapped in sweet potato dough and fried.

Beef noodles is a common lunch meal.

Family Roles

Family in Taiwan is not just a mother, a father, and their children. Family includes aunts and uncles, cousins, grandparents, and ancestors. Family roles are well established. Young family members typically show great respect for their elders, and grandparents are always honored.

A man plays with his son in Taiwan. Taiwanese fathers are becoming increasingly involved in taking care of their children.

Although Taiwan is a modern nation, fathers are still expected to be the main breadwinners. While fathers are the family earners, women have traditionally been the homemakers. Mothers were responsible for food, clothing, cleaning, and maintaining family ties. Wives were traditionally expected to obey their husbands and mothers-in-law. These rigid roles are changing as more women enter the workplace. As mothers are contributing to the family income, husbands are helping with school carpools, picking up groceries, and cleaning the house.

The pride of every family is its reputation. Parents seldom show anger toward their children in public. Parents try to persuade or encourage their children to behave appropriately. Public embarrassment is called "losing face." Taiwanese children learn at an early age not to cause their families to lose face.

A mother and daughter do errands on their scooter in Taipei. About half the women in Taiwan have jobs outside the home.

As Taiwan changes, its people look forward to greater personal freedom. At the same time, they look back at centuries of honoring family and ancestors. It is this blend of past, present, and future that gives Taiwan its distinct quality.

Timeline

TAIWAN HISTORY		WORLD HISTORY	
Ancient people build settlements on Taiwan.	10,000–500 BCE		
The Dapenkeng culture arises.	4000–3000 BCE		
		ca. 2500 BCE	The Egyptians build the pyramids and the Sphinx in Giza.
		ca. 563 BCE	The Buddha is born in India.
		313 CE	The Roman emperor Constantine legalizes Christianity.
		610	The Prophet Muhammad begins preaching a new religion called Islam.
		1054	The Eastern (Orthodox) and Western (Roman Catholic) Churches break apart.
		1095	The Crusades begin.
		1215	King John seals the Magna Carta.
		1300s	The Renaissance begins in Italy.
		1347	The plague sweeps through Europe.
Pirates occupy Taiwan.	1300s–1500s		
		1453	Ottoman Turks capture Constantinople, conquering the Byzantine Empire.
		1492	Columbus arrives in North America.
		1500s	Reformers break away from the Catholic Church, and Protestantism is born.
Portuguese sailors name the island Ilha Formosa.	1590		
The Dutch establish settlements on Taiwan.	1624		
Zheng Chenggong ousts the Dutch from Taiwan.	1661		
The Qing take over Taiwan.	1683		

TAIWAN HISTORY

Some Taiwan ports are opened for trade with foreign nations.	1858
Japan takes over Taiwan.	1895
At the end of World War II, Taiwan is returned to China.	1945
Chiang Kai-shek and two million Chinese retreat from China to Taiwan.	1949
Taiwan begins dynamic economic growth and trade.	1960
Chiang Kai-shek dies.	1975
The United States cuts off diplomatic ties with the Republic of China (Taiwan).	1979
The government ends martial law.	1987
A massive earthquake strikes central Taiwan, killing 2,415 people.	1999
Typhoon Morakot causes deadly landslides.	2009

WORLD HISTORY

1776	The U.S. Declaration of Independence is signed.
1789	The French Revolution begins.
1865	The American Civil War ends.
1879	The first practical lightbulb is invented.
1914	World War I begins.
1917	The Bolshevik Revolution brings communism to Russia.
1929	A worldwide economic depression begins.
1939	World War II begins.
1945	World War II ends.
1969	Humans land on the Moon.
1975	The Vietnam War ends.
1989	The Berlin Wall is torn down as communism crumbles in Eastern Europe.
1991	The Soviet Union breaks into separate states.
2001	Terrorists attack the World Trade Center in New York City and the Pentagon near Washington, D.C.
2004	A tsunami in the Indian Ocean destroys coastlines in Africa, India, and Southeast Asia.
2008	The United States elects its first African American president.

Fast Facts

Official name: Republic of China

Capital: Taipei

Official language: Mandarin Chinese

Taipei

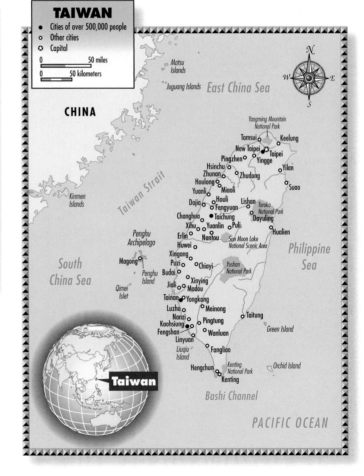

National flag

Official religion: None

National anthem: "Zhonghua Minguo guoge" ("National Anthem of the Republic of China")

Government: Multiparty democracy

Head of state: President

Head of government: Prime minister

Area of country: 13,855 square miles (35,884 sq km)

Highest elevation: Mount Yu, 12,966 feet (3,952 m) above sea level

Lowest elevation: Sea level along the coast

Largest lake: Riyue (Sun Moon) Lake, 3 square miles (8 sq km)

Tallest waterfall: Jiaolong, falls about 2,000 feet (600 m)

Longest river: Zhuoshui River, 116 miles (187 km)

Average daily high temperature: In Taipei, 66°F (19°C) in January; 94°F (34°C) in July

Average daily low temperature: In Taipei, 57°F (14°C) in January; 79°F (26°C) in July

Mount Yu

Taroko Gorge

Currency

National population (2013 est.):	23,299,716	
Population of major cities (2012 est.):	New Taipei	3,913,595
	Kaohsiung	2,773,885
	Taichung	2,662,770
	Taipei	2,647,122
	Tainan	1,876,706

Landmarks:

- ▶ *Kenting National Park*, Pingtung
- ▶ *Orchid Island*, off the southeast coast
- ▶ *Taipei night markets*
- ▶ *Taipei 101*, Taipei
- ▶ *Taroko Gorge*, near Hualien

Economy: Taiwan is the world's leading producer of laptop computers. It is also an important producer of electronics, chemicals, textiles, iron and steel, and machinery. Rice is the largest crop in Taiwan, but the country also produces abundant pineapples, mangoes, and cabbage. Hogs are the most valuable livestock. Chicken and cattle are also important.

Currency: The New Taiwan dollar. In 2013, 1 New Taiwan dollar equaled about 3 cents in U.S. currency, and 1 U.S. dollar equaled 30 New Taiwan dollars.

System of weights and measures: Taiwanese units and some metric units

Literacy rate: 96.1%

College students

Ang Lee

Common Mandarin Chinese words and phrases:

nihao	hello
huanying	welcome
zaoshang hao	good morning
wo henhao	I am fine
nihao ma?	How are you?
haixing	I'm OK
wo jiao…	My name is…
hen gaoxing jiandao ni	I am happy to meet you
qing ni	please
xiexie	thank you
zaijian	good-bye

Prominent Taiwanese people:

A-mei (1972–)
Singer

Chiang Kai-shek (1887–1975)
President

Chin-Feng Chen (1977–)
Baseball player

Cynthia Khan (1968–)
Martial arts actor

Huang Hai-tai (1901–2007)
Puppeteer

Ju Ming (1938–)
Sculptor and wood-carver

Ang Lee (1954–)
Academy Award–winning film director

Yani Tseng (1989–)
Golfer

To Find Out More

Books

▶ Chen, Jade, and Muriel Chen. *Blue Eye Dragon*. Sydney, New Holland Australia, 2008.

▶ Mills, Clifford W. *Ang Lee*. New York: Chelsea House, 2009.

▶ Yin Jia Min Zhu. *Chiang Kai-shek and Eight King Kongs*. Nanchang, China: 21st Century Publishing House, 2011.

DVDs

▶ *Crouching Tiger, Hidden Dragon*. Directed by Ang Lee. Culver City, CA: Sony Pictures, 2001.

▶ *Yi Yi*. Directed by Edward Yang. New York: Criterion, 2006.

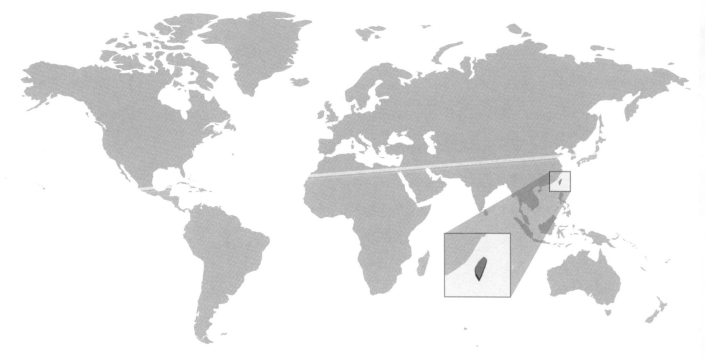

▶ Visit this Scholastic Web site for more information on Taiwan:
www.factsfornow.scholastic.com
Enter the keyword Taiwan

Index

Page numbers in *italics*
indicate illustrations.

Meet the Author

BARBARA SOMERVILL HAS BEEN WRITING CHILDREN'S nonfiction books for more than twenty years. She writes about countries, earth science, biographies, and social studies.

Somervill found writing about Taiwan to be a research adventure. For such a small island, there is abundant information available! She was lucky to find dozens of Taiwanese on the Internet who were gracious in telling her about their lives and their homeland. This was particularly true of Taiwanese high school students who were delighted to tell about their days, while practicing English.

Photo Credits